MUSTER

Written By

Jack Payne

Preface

Portland, Tennessee, is located between Bowling Green, KY, and Nashville, TN, about 30 miles either way. It is about 4 to 5 miles off what is now 1-65 and US 31W. SR109 and SR 52 are the main roads through town.

It was a small agricultural town producing mostly tobacco, wheat, corn, and later soybeans located on the Louisville & Nashville Railroad line. At least, that was the case until the thirties and forties when an enterprising and prosperous farmer named McGlothlin introduced strawberries to the town, making it the strawberry capital of the world. The cold temperatures of the north Highland rim in the early spring made it perfect and conducive to growing the fruit. The induction thrived and it took off to become an international market in production for the short season in the 40ies. My family shared in growing strawberries, and Dad had 5 acres or more most years. Today, the town (Portland) has a population of nearly 14,000 thousand, with 50% plus manufacturing jobs. In working hours between 8 to 5 PM, it becomes "blue collar heaven." One now would have to scrounge the area to find many growers that concentrate on raising just strawberries as their source of income.

This is a collection of stories of my life as I recall them at the age of 81 years. It is 85 to 90 percent truth, 15 percent names changed or altered to protect the dead, and then there is 5 percent considered pure "bull shit." That is my best trait! If I was not Irish, as Harry McGonigal coined, "I would be ashamed." I have had to wait until all my elder family members, neighbors, friends, strangers, even enemies, have passed on to attempt this effort. I surely hope retribution cannot be rendered from afar for any words written that might unintentionally offend anyone. My sincere hope for this effort is to bring some humor and some incite of growing up in a small rural farm town and having six older siblings that influenced me to be the best person. Welcome!

Merriam-Webster dictionary defines the word muster. Verb: To "bring together or to assemble troops." As a noun: Roll call or gathering roundup. Verline never knew how many eggs to fry in the morning until all her sons were downstairs. She never knew how many "strays," as she called them, that they brought home for the night. I chose Muster for the title. I was the youngest of six sons born to Verline and George Payne. I vividly recall, as a child, my father getting up very early. In the winter months, he would first make a rolling fire in the fireplace. He then tuned in the radio to 650 AM to check of any school closings or get the breaking news events. In the early years, I slept downstairs on a cot that was once the dining room and used as a day bed. While still under the covers keeping warm, I could easily hear the happenings going on. After heating the house, he would go to the stairwell door and holler upstairs to the brothers, "MUSTER." They dared not to hear the bellow out call more than once. As the boys dismounted, Mom is up now up and readying the kitchen for breakfast with a cozy fire in the Black Diamond stove. I was always the last to get up and I vaguely remember the stove. By now our house had been wired for electricity and replaced with carbide fixtures that lit our home and barn. Carbide lighting was considered very fashionable and not found often in the country. The carbide tank later served as our septic tank. The freeze of '51 that blanketed snow and iceparalyzed the county for weeks. Daddy brought the Black Diamond in from the cellar house and Mom cooked on it... She also cooked in the fireplace. I thought this was a treat before they reminded me it was the way of life just a few short years before. I would lay awake under the warm covers and listen ardently for the school closings, secretly praying that Sumner County would be on the list. This meant I could stay in bed a couple more hours. What fond memories of hearing the blasting radio. Starting in mid-December, commercials like "Escalators up and down, gifts on every floor, Harvey's has it, Harvey's has it, oh what fun it is to shop at Nashville largest store." This also meant yuletide music- Bill Monroe and his bluegrass band, "Christmas time a-coming" or Ernest Tubb, wailing out "Blue Christmas."

Muster

The word Muster was also adopted by brothers Tom, Jim, and Bobby after they had families and used it to get attention or be summoned by them. Jim was in the military for many years and used the term, but I am confident he remembered the early "greetings of the day" that G.W. imparted in all of us.

I use the word Muster, not only because of the memory of Dad getting my brothers up for the day but to draw an analogy. I have had to muster most of my life; live up to high standards set by my parents. Verline would beam proudly when she was told by teachers it was a pleasure having her sons as students or they were the most well-mannered in the class. She would also gloat that she raised seven children, and not one of them spent a night in jail. She went to her grave not knowing that in my Western Kentucky days, after a night of debauchery and drinking beer outside of Pure Truck Stop in dry Simpson County, KY., I spent a night in jail. The jailhouse is now a museum and archives center.

PORTLAND
TENNESSEE
Portland
IT'S WHERE MY STORY BEGINS

Chapter One:
May 23, 1943

In the month of May, the weather is normally hot and can be humid in middle Tennessee.. Today, the pomp and ceremony of the 87th Kentucky Derby "running for the roses" in Louisville had passed by two weeks; the 12th Iroquois Steeplechase in Belle Meade Nashville by a week. All outings and parties for best-dressed bid, tucker men, and broad brim hat ladies were now just memories and history for another year. The peonies, purple irises, and lilacs are, in perfusion, perfuming the air. It is strawberry picking time in Portland, TN. The 3000-plus town (pop. 1940) becomes a metropolis for two to three weeks in mid-May. Now, that depends on the amount of rainfall, as well as fending off late frosts. Both a lack of rain, excessive rainfall, or a killing frost can determine your entire crop yield for a year. The carnival is in town and shall bring out even the most reclusive and rural citizens of the county. My Uncle Evans used to question some of their "heritage" with good humor and secretly wondered how many were more than just cousins! Mr. Butt has been laboring for months doing construction on wagons and making every detail perfect on each float in hopes to win the prize as most beautiful. Beautiful young girls are making last-minute adjustments to their formal gowns to ride on floats that will proceed down Broadway. Adding to that will be the 101st Army band and color guard from Ft. Campbell, KY, Al Menah Shrine Temple from Nashville with their troops of clowns, musicians, motorbikes, and an entire parade guard. Legions of bands come from neighboring high schools and colleges that vie to be the loudest and best. The bets are always on Nashville A & I University (now TSU) marching band to get the coveted first prize. Most people have money in their pockets because they have aligned themselves with the strawberry production season and have come near and far to Portland to make money. The weather today is fabulous with low humidity and loaming fluffy gray clouds.

Daddy, Uncle Jim, plus most of my brothers- Fred, Harold, Jim, and Bob, were coaxing Dave and Elick, our stubborn and probably exhausted mules, through the dog trot of our cattle barn. Several neighbors were also present either at the barn or yard. I visited Arnold Pirtle in Gallatin and got some facts from his account of the day. He now lives in Stevensville, Montana, with his son Ralph. (Note: Arnold recently passed and is buried in Chicago with his wife Barbara, Apr 23) I recently talked to him on his 95th birthday. He and I are the last from the "ole guard Austin neighborhood." He, Ms. Emma, and Mr. Ernest were there helping with the strawberry harvest. The berries had to be culled and assorted by size, crated and then be ferried by truck for the four-mile trek to the train station in Portland. Daddy was balancing his time between a very anxious wife who was about to give birth to their seventh child and overseeing his "berry empire." It is Las Vegas in Portland, and the strawberries are the "gold."

Expounding further on that Sunday of May 23, 1943, it was probably the second to third week of the berry season. It peaks differently every year with the spring cold temperatures. Most of the farmers usually would not "pick" on Sunday, but the berries have a short threshold to stay on the vine. People are tired, but rise to the occasion and are secretly are ready for the season to be over.

I was born at home as were my previous siblings. It was still popular to give birth at home. Mom's distant cousin on the John's side, Nora Stewart, was imported from Nashville for the berry season to babysit and help cook for the "hands." Today, she is acting as a midwife. Nora seemed to be more a thorn in my parent's side than help, but she showed up like clock-work every May if I remember. Nora had her leg amputated (something to do about chasing a boy) at a very early age, but that didn't seem to slow her down one bit. She loved Marty Robbins, embellishing truths to the point that it was not feasible. She would sit up until the wee hours listening to the radio WSM blasting loudly. Mom and Dad would try to get some sleep in the adjoining room for the grinding next day that came at daylight. Finally, Dad would scream, "Nora, turn off that damn radio and go to bed!" I always thought Nora was worldly and sophisticated. Mom was always thrilled when she went home to Nashville! Long before we had air conditioning, a bed had been set up in the living room and next to the south window for the delivery. This room offered the best cross ventilation with the windows of our house that were set high on our property on Old Gallatin Road. It also served as a sitting room for visitors to visit the new baby. There was almost always a breeze in our yard, even in August, but brutally cold in the winter. Waiting in the center hall of the barn, the mules were beginning to relax, knowing it was the last run for the day. They were a direct shot, about 300 feet away, to the living room window where my mother lay in labor. The barnyard was separated by a freshly painted, white picket fence from our yard. It was mating season on the farm; anxious chickens and an amorous roaster were cavorting in the loft. At the height of passion, an excited hen lost her footing, dropping below between the startled mules. The mules took off full throttle, strewing baskets of fruit in every direction. They sailed out at full pace, tearing down the freshly painted fence, and headed directly toward the window. Frozen in awe, someone on the porch was screaming and waving trying to distract the thundering herd to stir away from their path of destruction. The yoke between them extended at least two feet in front of them. It was the perfect missile to come through the window. Someone threw an object, perhaps a yard rake, to divert them within three feet of hitting the house or crashing through the window. The velocity of the turn forced the rear of the wagon to slam into the house, ripping off shingles and thrusting the yolk of the wagon to lodge in a fork in a nearby peach tree. It stopped the mules but also dumped the last of the berries all over the yard. Impending death was averted, and I came out healthy and screaming, I'm told, a little past 5 PM… and to my knowledge, the nervous Doctor never visited our house again. Mom was also okay as it was an easy birth after delivering six other children. I'm not sure if Dad made it to the train station with his cargo that day or not. I believe it was proof that a guardian angel averted the tragedy when I was just minutes old. That divine assurance has kept me from harm's way on many occasions since. When I feel I'm in peril, I rely on that peace of mind that everything will be okay. But for the sake of the book, I am also still screaming.

Chapter Two: Early Years

I came from artistic genes. Family talents were both musical and artistic. I assume it was derived from Irish genes. My grandmother had a pump organ in her home. She boarded the traveling (male) music teacher for lessons for her seven children. This was commendable for a widow for fear of scandal, to house an unmarried man in their home in that era. Most of my mother's siblings could play the instrument. There was also always a piano and live song in our home. My first and last singing performance was near the age of four. Listening (circa 1949) WSM radio, I sang the entire lyrics of "SHAME, SHAME ON YOU" along with Red Foley and the Lawrence Welk Orchestra. To date, I still cannot carry a tune, but my favorite genres of music are Country and Big Band Orchestras. Nashville has an American Song Book station.

I was about three or four, and my nearly blonde curly locks were making me look more like a girl than a boy. The beanie cap and short pants with a jacket didn't help my image either. It was decided that my brother Tom and sister Ann would take me to the barbershop. I don't remember it much, but I have been told I showed my ass out in Mr. Reddick's barber shop on Main Street. They were trying their best to appease and bribe me as best they could. When he turned on the buzzing clippers and draped the cloth around me, I went ballistic. Tom was mortified with embarrassment, I'm sure. For years later and in my teens, when I passed the shop on the main street, I got lumps in my stomach and could not look Mr. Reddick in the face.

My earliest artistic recall was with my maternal Great Aunt Etta Brawner. She was a gifted artist and I hated her as a child. She lived with my Aunt Minnie (Denning) and Uncle Bill Johns. She seemed to dislike children. I guess she felt exiled and bitter toward life. I was probably five when a death in the family took Mom and Dad out of town. I'm not sure where Bobby stayed; he was 10 or 11, and perhaps he went with them. I was relegated to stay with Uncle

Bill and Aunt Minnie. They were newly married and lived on Morningside Drive in Portland. I remember him picking me up in a near new model T Ford, and I thought I was headed for a great time. Upon arrival there lay in residence, Aunt Etta. Things went seemingly well for an eternity in my young mind, with Uncle Bill and Ant Minnie humoring me. I wasn't so fortunate with Aunt Etta. Considering I was spoiled rotten and had never been away from my parents, I coped. Aunt Etta, trying to appease me with a gesture of peace offering to seek my good favor, painted a beautiful red cardinal. I remember taking it, wadding it up, throwing it in defiance at her. I am sure my parents were told of my insolence. I don't remember what punishment I received. I would treasure that piece of artwork today. Aunt Etta probably loathed me even more after that. I paid for that indiscretion for years. As a child, I had chronic throat problems. My ailments were always worse in winter. When a student at Portland Elementary, grades first through fifth, we rode a late bus route home. On many rainy days, probably due to boredom and anxiety, I would be outside, sloshing through the water puddles and getting drenched. Mom constantly badgered my older brothers to watch over me and see that I stayed inside. They wanted nothing to do with monitoring their little brother. It also didn't cause goodwill with teachers with Mom as she thought they should monitor me more closely. She thought I would grow out of it, but it plagued me for years. A young boy that was my age that they knew died on the operating table from a botched tonsillectomy. That sealed the deal for me not to have the surgery. Years later, when I was a freshman at the University of Tennessee Nashville, I blacked out and was taken to Vanderbilt Hospital for an emergency tonsillectomy. Dr. Rosenblum performed and became my PC Doctor for years. Now, let's get back to Aunt Etta.

Aunt Etta's favorite color was lavender. When she died, I was 9 years old. The body was laid out in Uncle Bill and Aunt Minnie's living room. She was in a lavender and purple felt casket and a lavender shroud with banks and banks of purple and white flowers surrounding the casket. Aunt Blanche and Uncle Boy Johns had endless gardens of purple irises and white peonies in full bloom in their gardens. Ms. Una Mae Gregory at the Flower Basket had artfully arranged the flowers into beautiful arrangements. This site image plagued me for years. I had convulsions in my throat with raging temperatures every wintertime. One particular time, I had a nightmare, and my fever had to be in the 100-plus range. The Vick wax and flannel cloth that was Dr. Verline didn't heal me this time. I am not going to say that I died, but I am told when you do, there is an iridescent light that is more illuminated than you could ever paint. At the peak of my illness, I saw a lighted sky and, lo and behold, Santa Claus blazing across the sky and, in the rear of the sled, a toy chest. In the chest, Aunt Etta's purple casket, along with the purple flowers festooning her casket and flailing through the sky. I woke up, and my fever had peaked. I ate like a horse at breakfast. I continued to have throat problems but never had a negative thought about my Aunt Etta again, and I was told years later by a therapist that it was my childhood self-conscience that released the negative energy of Aunt Etta. Go figure!

Not all my youth experiences were negative. There were frequent shopping excursions to Nashville. This usually involved the entire day. Long before Interstate 65, it normally took nearly an hour to reach downtown. Cain Sloan, Caster Knott, and Harveys were the major department stores. Harveys was Mom's favorite, spanning an entire city block, and was 5 or 6 stories high. It was the first store in Nashville to have escalators. It was not as toney as the others, and my mom was in heaven to get to the bargain basement...much like Felines in Boston. Owner Fred Harvey was a product from Marshall Field in Chicago and knew well how to market his wares. His trademark was carousel horses, and they were prominently displayed on every level and branded on gift boxes and advertisements. On the fifth floor was Max. He commanded the monkey bar and carousel ride. He was a very kind older man and probably of Russian descent. He had an endless amount of patience and seemed to thrive entertaining children for hours and hours... Mom would deposit me at the monkey bar, and she and Ann would disappear for hours. This would never, ever fly in today's culture. First, PETA wouldn't tolerate monkeys in a cage.

Secondly, no way Max could have monitored 20 or more children without one of them being abducted. This was an all-day affair; we usually lunched at the B &W cafeteria or sometimes at the white table-clothed Cross Keys on Capital Blvd. Being a child, I usually got anxious after several hours of traipsing around from store to store, and I was usually bribed that we would eat at a Krystal before the journey home. There were several located downtown. Krystals were .5 cents each, and even then, at age 5 or 6, I could pack away 4 or 5. At the end of the day, all three of us were exhausted; we would make our way back to Cain Sloan to their valet parking garage. I usually fell asleep on the way back, having tried to stay awake to throw an apple core out the window crossing the Cumberland River. It didn't take much then to entertain me.

Wintertime was always a festive time. When I was four or five, I remember the aroma of my mother baking tea cakes. Daddy would be stripping tobacco in the Old Austin School building which was located where Bobby's house now sits. The property reverted to our farm property after the new school was built across the street. Daddy made the old abandoned schoolhouse into a stripping house, and it held forth until a tornado took it down, probably in the early 50s. Anyway, she would box up a pan of cakes and direct me to deliver them to him. She would stand in the doorway to make sure I made the passage safely. I can still smell those ginger tea cakes.

In January 1951, my Aunt Berley Scott's twins, Jack and Jill, were born; I was nearly eight years old. There was a major nor'easter snow and freeze to hit Portland and middle Tennessee. We were without electric power for weeks, and there were several deaths. We were fortunate that Uncle Evans Johns had a 1948 Willis Jeep and could navigate the roads. For me, it was an adventure. Daddy sat up the old Black Diamond cooking store that had been relegated to the cellar house, put it back up in the kitchen, taking out a window panel to let the smoke escape. Mama also cooked in the fireplace in the living room with cast iron pots and skillets. They dragged out the kerosene lanterns that had been in storage for years. I also vividly recall, at the age of 48, she getting in a corn scoop in our sloping front yard and sliding all the way down Old Gallatin Road to near the Pirtle's house with me draped around her shoulders.

Another time in the early spring, Mom, Ann, and I had been on a shopping trip to Nashville. One of my brothers, perhaps Jim, had plowed up a rabbit hatch and found an infant bunny. Anticipating our arrival, one of the boys put the rabbit underneath a soup bowl on the kitchen floor. Daddy coaxed me to pick up the bowl and see the surprise. I stared in awe at the bunny, and after a long silence, Mom said, "Oh, that poor rabbit has lost its mother!" To everyone's dismay, I started screaming and throwing a hissy fit as to why they would have brought the rabbit to the house. Everybody was furious at Mom for broaching the fact that the rabbit had been orphaned. Bob was the most pissed because he had to take the bunny back in the dark near where it had been dislodged. There was not much conversation at dinner that night, but it was the start of me being an animal activist and not even being able to kill a Bambi or hunt in general. Now, opossums, squirrels, and raccoons, trust me that is a different subject when it comes to my vegetable garden!

Christmases for me as a child growing up were magical. Mother always baked and cooked for days. We always had the prettiest lighted Christmas tree in the neighborhood. The mantel over the fireplace is decorated with greens and ribbon with cedar boughs over the window and door frames. One year, probably six, I received a Nichol Plate Road 956 train set. It was sat up around the base of a table in the living room. Ann got a beautiful white chenille bathrobe that she had hinted at for weeks. When she opened the box, she put on the robe and started whirling around in glee. Wrapping papers were fanned, and the now-dry tree caught on fire. A couple of brothers grabbed the tree, a couple of brothers grabbed Ann, and all ran out into the snow. The tree was destroyed but it was always taken down the day after anyway. When I got older, this was always a bone of contention with me and my parents to take it down so soon, but I'm sure they remember when the house almost when up in flames from the dry tree. I now leave my tree up sometimes until March or after. Ann didn't salvage her robe that memorable Christmas morning, but my train escaped ruin, and I still have it displayed over windows in my Florida room.

I had a privileged (spoiled) childhood to be from a poor country folk family. I say poor, but we were rich. Always with a cellar full of canned goods, a smokehouse of three butchered hogs, a pen full of chickens, ducks swimming on the pond, and guineas and peacocks wandering the 45 yards.

It was almost as if my parents raised two families. Anna, my sister, was 20 years and one month older. She was well out of high school (class of '41 SCHS). She already had a job at General Shoe Corp in Gallatin. This later let her move to Nashville and work for the CEO, Maxie Jarman. With his influence, later, she furthered her career in Washington D.C., working in the Pentagon for the Chief of Naval Operations. George Thomas (Tom), my oldest brother, was 18 and preparing for a tour with the US Army in Germany. He quit high school his senior year to join the cold war of WW2 but returned after his hitch to graduate with SCHS, Class of 1948. My siblings, including Bob, who was five years old, would attest that they had been too rough growing up. This time was of the Depression era, and everything was tight for most everyone. My family was far from being rich, but I had it much better than many. My parents were enterprising; we had a working farm and a large orchard that brought in revenue. Never, ever, were we without food or resorted to wearing patched clothes. The clothes were also clean. We had wonderful neighbors who were more like family and could barter with them. We had a reliable vehicle, attended church, and had God in our hearts. Austin School was across the road from our house, so the sibs could never use the "I had to walk five miles to school" bit. Ann had her white high heel pumps and gold graduation ring, just like the "rich" kids in town. A line from *Cold Miner's Daughet,* "Daddy always got the money somewhere," applied to us. Daddy might have had to sell a hog and rely on his tobacco or strawberry crop. Mom would sell eggs or a bushel of apples, but they also provide well. Now, I must say rather than one or two wool sweaters, I probably had five or six to choose from to wear to school. This is just an example of how I had it easier but had older brothers and sisters to help with the household expenses. Harold and Fred were already working good-paying jobs by the time I was age ten. Mom and Dad were the first to have a television and indoor plumbing in our neighborhood. I have a vague memory of the outhouse, but there was one at my grandmother's for several years. With only one channel to watch, the neighbors would flock to our house to watch TV regularly. Mom would always have homemade tomato juice and popcorn. During the cold, long winter months, there were always card games every Saturday night and, in summer, croquet Sunday games on our neatly mowed lawn. Many Sundays, Uncle Fred and Aunt Catherine would drive up from Nashville with most of their seven children. Dad and Uncle Fred could behead a chicken blindfolded. Aunt Catherine could have taught Colonel Sanders a thing or two about frying chicken. Combine this with my mother's banana pudding; it was "Bill of Fare at the Ritz" dining.

Mother was the main dispenser of punishment. Usually, a fierce stare could do the trick, but it could up the game with a shrill shriek that meant business. She never used the one, two, or three methods. The only time I remember my dad whipping me, I was about 9. Ann had Italian friends visiting Nashville from Boston. She wanted to show them that we could make spaghetti and meatballs as good as they could. She scrubbed and probably repainted the dining room. Out came a red and white checkered tablecloth plus white cloth napkins. She was even allowed to have port wine served in stemmed wine glasses. I was totally caught up in this "worldliness." I demanded to sit at the dining table. I was told more than once that my seating was at the little people's table in the kitchen. As dinner hour approached, I wrapped myself around the center post of the dining table. That table is now in the home of my nephew Tom. Daddy was probably more flustered with how to wrap pasta around a spoon as Ann had drilled him, the cloth napkins, and be on best manners for the Italians. After a couple of polite "Jackie, get out from under the table" all hell broke loose. He yanked me out from under the table, led me out the back door, and snatched a limb off an Elm tree. He proceeded to wear my ass out behind the smokehouse. I was banished immediately to bed and never got to taste the spaghetti or see the Italians off. I guess Mom learned the art of continental cooking because it became one of our go-to meals for years. Ann was furious with me and didn't speak to me for at least a week.

Growing up in the country, I had limited playmates. I was deprived of groups like the Cub or Boy Scouts and little league ball teams. I was subjected more to older neighbors and my parent's friends. I always had a rapport with adults from my childhood and could converse on their level. I guess some would say I was precocious. My earliest childhood friend was Glen Groves. He was in walking range and lived nearer to Hwy 52 on Payne Road. It was Halloween Eve; we were probably eight or nine, and I was spending the night. His parents were going to the funeral home for a wake, leaving us alone. Prior to their leaving, we proceeded to block the road with everything we could find. We were watching from a field as his father cursed every time he had to stop to unclog the road. Glen thought he would be punished when they returned home, but it was never mentioned, and I was never invited back. Another childhood friend was Billy Freedle. He would sometimes accompany us on some of the Nashville trips. One year, he thinks we were eight or nine, we went to the State Fair. We went into the haunted house. We became paralyzed with fear, and after cowering in the dark for at least thirty minutes, Mom had the operator turn on the lights and come to retrieve us. She was more embarrassed than we were scared.

Another childhood memory was visiting my Aunt Berley and Uncle Willie Grey's house in Robertson County at the Cook farm. They had ten children, and it was always a treat to go visit them. The kids were playing in the yard, and I was pulling a wagon with a rake. Somehow, I fell over the rake handle and broke my left arm. It was badly broken at the wrist. It was Sunday afternoon, and that was pre-cell phones. Thank God Anna was with us and rode in the back seat to Simonton's Clinic in Portland. I don't know who was more excited, Dad or Mom. Ann was trying to keep all three of us calm. In the fray, someone had called the Doctor because he was waiting for us when we arrived. I had a heavy cast to start the fourth grade, and it also made for a good icebreaker in Ms. Bigbee's class.

PAYNE HOMEPLACE

Chapter Three: Teen Years and SCHS

I was fourteen when Bobby graduated from SCHS Class of '57. He and I always had a bittersweet relationship. We worked closely together and years later for Bel Air Studios. We were "oil and vinegar" when spending too much time together. We could share very cutting words but would defend each other to death if challenged. Our other bond was inherited, probably from our Veteto genes. It was our insatiable wit. We could feed off each other and have scenarios that professional comics could not do. We could pick out people, anybody. Without being mean-spirited or cruel, I could pin a pet name on them and, most times, always agree it fit. My family, for generations, has always had pet names for most everyone they knew. Not cruel or mean-spirited names. After I grew up, we became closer. He let me drive his 1962 Chevrolet car to the prom, and I was honored to serve at his 1970 wedding to Gloria Stone of Lafayette. He always had my back.

I could not have been more excited than the day I turned sixteen. I was eligible for an intermediate restricted driver's license. Now, this privilege was not to allow me to "run the streets" but to put another driver in the house. Bob had already left the house, and this would provide more freedom for Mom. I drove to the National Guard Amory that day and memorized the manual. It was a sure thing. Even though I was nervous, I mastered the writing and conquered the driving requirements. I can't recall what model vehicle we had in '59, but Dad always had a fairly new car. The trooper complimented me on my skills as he walked to the rear of the car to record the plate number. To my dismay, the rear license plate had come off and was nowhere to be seen. The trooper would not approve my license. I sensed he felt my anxiety but was professional. My parents had gotten me out of school that afternoon to take me to Gallatin. The courthouse would be closing within minutes. Daddy couldn't locate the registration for the vehicle, and we were sent packing. This meant having to wait another two weeks without me being allowed to drive. I probably didn't cry, but very few words were spoken on the long ride back to Portland.

Robert (Bob) Phillips, my second cousin, lived in San Francisco. He came to live at Grandma's and Uncle Evans during my junior year in high school. Bob was six months older than me, but it was like having another brother that year in 1960. He and I didn't always share the same interests. He was more worldly and smarter than me. Latin and Mathematics were a total breeze for him. His passion was archery range. It had to be a culture shock for him to come to Tennessee. There wasn't a bathroom at Grandma's, and he was relegated to the upstairs. It was unheated and not insulated from the elements. He had to walk the mile on Buntin Mill Road to catch the school bus. Despite our differences, it was a joy to have him. He would often spend the night and get off the bus at my house after school. He later lived for a short time with Aunt Velma and Amelia Ann in Nashville. That fall, I started school at Draughons in Nashville. He and I would share several antics staying out all night, clubbing in Printers Alley, or God knows what else. He was admonished often by Aunt Velma for fear of retaliation from Verline for leading me down a "sinful path." Bob and Sherry now live in coastal Oregon, and I have had wonderful visits with them and their beloved Blue.

It was early March 1960, my junior year. Ann, with my parents, picked me up at school. I had no idea why but reasoned it was bad news. I didn't find out until we were on our way that my dear brother Harold had been shot. Harold was the third son of George and Verline. (He was the type of brother that, at probable age ten, me crying and pouting, going to bed early on the 4th of July because I didn't have fireworks, would get me up and go to a mart and spend a lot of money to appease me.) He had movie star looks and talent to match. He was a gifted singer and was musical from an early age. It was said that he wouldn't participate in Ms. Stinson's piano recital because she wouldn't allow him to play "Piano roll blues"! Tom and Harold both had taken lessons from Ms. Lizzie. After Hume Fogg, cousin Billy enlisted in the Navy. Harold had sights set far from Portland and, to my parents' dismay, quit his senior year of high school to join the Navy. He already had his SCHS, Class of '52 class, photographs taken at Mr. Stark's studio.

His quitting school had a positive note. He was stationed mostly in the Pacific and was lucky to see Billy and Cousin Dorothy often when in port in California. His musical skills allowed him into the Special Forces. He formed a band and toured ship to ship, entertaining the sailors. He had honed his talent and, when discharged, returned to the stateside to make his mark as an entertainer. Fred was already establishing himself in Louisville, KY. This was prior to his establishing Bel Air Studios. They both worked at various jobs and played music on the weekends. Very talented as well, Fred didn't want to pursue the music dream as strongly as Harold. Harold lived and breathed music. This was the beginning of rockabilly; hardcore country (hillbilly) was not in style, except on the Grand Ole Opry. Harold was too smooth for that style and was ahead of his time. He had always cut some songs at Star Day Studios on Dickerson Pike in Nashville. Two songs of note: "I'll Miss You Tomorrow" and "Honkytonk Stomp," were written by him. He played and starred at several Louisville venues, and this led to an early morning show on WAVE television. Harold made acquaintances with several people who were trying to make it in the business. Roger Miller, then unknown, from Oklahoma, was seeking his dream, too. He would taunt Harold about being from Nashville, living in Louisville, and wanting to be in music. Roger moved to Nashville, was a bellhop at one of the major hotels (the Andrew Jackson) site of the Tennessee Performance Arts Center, met the right connection, was pitched "King of the Road," and the rest is history. This was just months after Harold died. He died far too soon not to have seen the stardom that he so ardently pined for.

One year, he, Sunny Dull, Sarah Keeney, and two or three other female singers came down for the annual Disc Jockey (now CMA) Convention. Murfreesboro Road then had perhaps twenty or more motels and motor lodges. There was the Colony, the Mercury, Howard

Johnsons, and many more. Anyway, arriving in town in one of the girls' pink Cadillac convertibles, they needed a place to freshen up and change clothes. Not a necessary place to sleep as they would be up all night, mingling with the stars, before driving back to Louisville. Anyway, as the story goes, one of the girls went in to inquire about a room. She explained they simply needed a room to change, and there would be no hanky-panky! The clerk could clearly see the pink Cadillac and Harold with a harem of girls! The flustered lady said she would have to converse with her husband in a back room. He, hard of hearing, kept asking her what the matter was. At the top of her lungs, she finally said: "It's some of that Ole Red Foley bunch wanting to shack up!" Clearly, country music has come a long way with acceptance.

As his star rose, so did his fan base. His Hollywood good looks and charm drew a lot of female followers. His discretion was not always good in his choice of suitors. While he dated respectable ladies, one I shall not name was bad news. He was trying to ease out of the relationship. She was indebted to him, perhaps had one of his musical instruments. He called to say that he was stopping by to retrieve his property. She was defiant he had not come to her house. Strong-willed and determined, he proceeded to her house anyway. She had called an ex-lover, Eugene Younger, who was out of jail or prison on parole, to thwart Harold's request. An engaging conversation ensued, and according to reports, Harold stated he didn't want any trouble; he was shot in the abdomen. Harold lay there in his blood for a lengthy time before she called Fred and told him what had happened. Fred called the police, and Harold was rushed to the General Hospital. Ashamed, embarrassed, and hoping he would recover, Fred waited two days to call home. This was after Cousin Lillie Bowe confronted Fred at the hospital and warned him, "You have 15 minutes to call home, or I am going to." He called home, and we were on the road within an hour. Dad was concerned about him being at a mercy hospital, but the surgeons told him he was at Louisville's best for a gunshot wound. I was able to visit him briefly. He was conscious and wanted to know how school was. He was very ashamed around Mom and constantly would say, "What will Grandma think"? My parents were stoic, reassuring to him around him, but it was clear he was in bad condition. There were simply too many of his organs that had been penetrated. He being a known celebrity, the media made a field day of it. "Hillbilly singer shot."

A record snow hit Tennessee on March 3rd, 1960. Wilkinson Wiseman somehow made it to KY to pick up Harold. Jim, in the Air Force in Germany, switched flights from Louisville to Nashville. Marge had come down from Michigan. Thomas C. was on a work site and immediately came to Louisville to meet Ann. It was a nightmare getting home. Interstate 65 had not been completed, and we were stuck on a hill in E town for hours. The trip took 9 to 10 hours. Uncle Boy had the road crew bulldoze snow from Highway 52 all the way to our house. It was probably three AM before we got to our driveway. This was before (Old Gallatin Rd) Payne Road had been paved. Evans, Uncle Boy, Blanche, and several others had the fireplace blazing and food galore. The house was spic and span. The rest is a mere faded memory-but on Saturday Night, Grant Turner on the Grand Ole Opry acknowledged Harold, extending sympathy to his grieving family. That was the closest he made it to celebrity. He was sorely missed by everyone who knew him, and my mother was never, ever the same. She cried and often rarely smiled, and her personality became negative.

Her overprotective nature affected me as well. This also increased her protective mothering measures, particularly to me, which she never showed my older brothers. That hovering sometimes was so strict that I was not allowed to spread my wings. I resented it vehemently.

My teen years were typical for being raised on a farm. Dad never insisted very much I work in the fields, and certainly, I didn't have the father-son bond my older brothers shared. They had to work in the fields. I was more of a Mama's boy and had to do work around the house. Dad worked like a Trojan horse and seemed to do better alone. Now, don't get me wrong, I had work chores to do before any television and certainly had my fill of setting, chopping, suckering, and cutting tobacco. I also worked in the strawberry fields from weeding, mulching, and picking. Other chores were doing the evening milking and bringing in kindling for Dad to start the morning fire in the grate. It was always toasty warm when I got up in the morning.

Our relationship changed later in life as Dad got old and I was mature. It was me that had to take away his independence to drive. Daddy became a terror behind the wheel. He would run red lights, tail gate, cut people off, and drive on the wrong side of the road. It became a joke in town, "Watch out, here comes Mr. George." It's a miracle he did not kill someone.

I drove him to all his doctor's appointments. Sometimes, the Doctor would say, "Is this your Grandson?" Dad would say proudly, "This is my son." One of my fondest memories I have was a hot summer day, when we were passing the beer joints on 31W. Dad said, "Let's stop in at Wallace's and have a cold beer." That moment was worth a hundred fishing trips I never had with my father.

High school years were normal and routine for being raised in the country. It meant I missed a lot of school activities. We didn't have a school band, and I didn't play football. I did play basketball my freshman year, but I was not very good at sports. Plus, there was a transportation challenge, having to practice after school. Mom didn't drive and Dad would be working in the fields.

Our class had somewhat of a caste mentality. You might say, "the haves and have-nots." I was popular pretty much with all. I was friends with the "moneyed" group as well as those who had little or nothing at home. Verline always made that paramount, "By the grace of God, go I." I was neither ever better nor less off than anyone. After nearly 60 years, SCHS, Class of '61, some of the under-achiever classmates became the most successful. We have remained a close-knit class, and many of us still get together. In my last year, I was in the senior play. It was Mr. Beane from Lima. I was Berley Bickford

Beane. In the lead part, I played a gangly, nerdish Englishman, a want-to-be novelist. It gave me the acting bug, and later, I was in a couple of productions that Western Players at Western Ky University produced. I guess that set precedence, as I later became a professional photographer that required a lot of animation to get the perfect shot.

The late summer of 1949 saw nearly 100 war babies enrolled at Portland Elementary School. Portland's school system was not adequately able to handle the influx of students. Ms. Frankie Dye was added to the roster and jumped a grade with us every year. I was fortunate to have her for two years and accredit her as a good role model for a teacher. As of November 2023, there were 39 surviving from a class of 89 that walked across that stage of June 1961. I wasn't a disciplined student in school. I guess I had ADHD, but in 1949, it wasn't diagnosed. Therefore, going to college was not a prerequisite.

Chapter Four: College

I never fully applied myself in high school to maintain excellent grades. I guess I probably suffered a form of ADHD, but it wasn't called that then. As long as I maintained a C average, my parents didn't harass me much. It was demanded of me to finish high school and my parents wanted me to go to college. Even at an early age, I was more interested in the arts, theatre, and travel. I did well in English and American and World history. Algebra and Calculus bored me to death, and I simply wasn't interested. Because of my average grades, I didn't pursue to attend a major university. It was decided that I would attend Draughons Business College, now University, on 8th Avenue in Nashville. Billy also decided to attend so that sealed the deal. Ms. Russell had a large house on Richland Ave, a block off West End Avenue. She was a feisty, midseventies, opinionated lady who fought with everyone unless they were Church of Christ or born west of West High School. She was bitter about almost everything and could curse like a sailor and tell very vulgar jokes. She hated all the neighbors, and they hated her. She referred to one as "more pricks have died in her ass than on the battlefield at Shiloh." That wasn't exactly the vernacular I was used to being from Payne Road in Portland. She had maybe 8 to 10 boys as boarders, and most of them attended either Falls or Draughons school. She would talk badly about them behind their backs and how some of them lacked social graces and came from far beneath her social standing. She met her match with Verline when I moved in. The only room left available was in the basement. The plumbing pipes were exposed on the ceiling; the furnace was next to the bed, and cobwebs were everywhere with exposed rock foundation walls. That was the main decor, and was an invitation for brown recluse spiders and snakes. Billy was assigned to the second floor, and I was assigned to the dungeon. Verline let her know quickly and under no uncertain terms that I would not be in a dank basement. It seemed alright with Ms. Richards to let me go until Mom said firmly: "If Jackie goes, so does Billy." As we were the last crop of victims that the school would be sending, she couldn't bear the fact of losing two renters. Apologetically, she said I would probably be happier upstairs, and she would relocate one of the boys. Poor Herman came from rural Livingston and didn't have a choice but to go to the basement. She joked later that he barely had shoes when he came, and the basement was a palace to what he was used to at home. Breakfasts were worse than boot camp. You never knew what her demeanor would be. She would slap half-cooked eggs and bacon on your plate, and you dared not challenge her style. I finally got enough of her boot camp and moved over one block on West End Avenue to Ms. Nichols.

Ms. Nichols was a scone of old Nashville society. She was in good standing with the Downtown Presbyterian Church, and all her children went to the best colleges and had thriving careers. She maintained her status with the elite and was one of the classiest ladies I ever met. Her four-story mansion is still one of the grandest on The West End. Her husband was involved in a sensationalized murder that played out for a year with the Nashville Banner and Tennessean. Money couldn't reprieve him, and she visited him regularly at the TN State Prison. She never divulged any details. I visited her years later after I was working and making a good salary and I had purchased Maui Manner. She was as gracious as when I rented a room from her. She asked about every detail about my house and my favorite room. I described my Florida room, now the office, that it was white, powder blue, chartreuse, and yellow. At Christmas time that year, I received in the mail a needle-pointed stocking. Colors: yellow, powder blue, white, and chartreuse. I still hang it every Christmas. I shall always remember raiding her fridge at night and thinking she didn't know. She knew and never said a word.

Before I graduated from Draughons, I had multiple jobs. My first job was sacking groceries at H G Hills on Nolensville Pike. Many stars like Porter Wagon, Web Pierce, and Marty Robbins shopped there, and we had "sack to car" delivery. I would wheel their cart of groceries to their cars and Marty, sometimes Porter, would usually tip

$5.00. That was like $20.00 in 1961. My second job was as a billing clerk at Thurston Motor Lines on Murfreesboro Rd.

Later, I worked for an architect that was developing the Knob Hill Rd area in Belle Meade. The WSM studios were being built right down from the $500,000 homes that are now worth a million or more. It was at this time I met the Ragsdales (Ray Stevens) from Snellville, GA. This was before "Ahab the Arab" had hit the charts. I was still very immature and didn't know what I wanted to do with the rest of my life. The selective service was active (Vietnam was being stirred up), but as long as I was taking college courses at the University of TN, Nashville, I was exempt from the call. I quit school in early '64, and to my great surprise, I immediately received a letter that opened with GREETINGS.

Chapter Five: Military

The official letter from Uncle Sam arrived sometime in early May, prior to my birthdate. I guess the initial impact of how my life was going soon to change forever didn't fully register. However, the closer it came down to the wire that I was going to report for basic training in early June, broached a lot of family conversation. I had dropped out of classes at UTN, was 21, healthy, but totally not focused on a career. The draft was in full recruitment mode. I actually was looking forward to a new adventure. My father had served proudly in World War I in France as a medic; all five of my brothers had served in the military. Why should I not? The brothers tried to and did instill the fear of death in me. I was gangly, sissified, and had been pampered. I was tall, skinny, and still had lots of sickly issues at the age of 21. There was absolutely no assurance when my brothers, and in front of me no less, would chant, "Daddy, call somebody. We got to get him out of the army. They will kill him in basic training!" He had been on more than a speaking basis with Senator Al Gore, father of Vice President Al Gore of Carthage. They said, "Call Uncle Al and get him out." They, being their baby brother protectors, drilled constantly, keep your mouth shut. Under absolutely no circumstances do you ever volunteer for anything and keep a low profile. Hopefully, you won't get killed! My Dad, to their protest, would say, "Jackie will be fine." Finally, the day arrived, and Mom and Dad drove me down to Gallatin to the old post office building to check in for the bus ride to the Noel Hotel in Nashville. There, we would spend the night before boarding a Delta flight the next morning to Columbia, S.C. via Atlanta. This era was prior to segregation, and I was always taught to be respectful and kind to everyone. Other than Ms. Ivy, who worked at Grandma's and occasionally for us, I simply didn't have a lot of black people connections. Mama dispersing last-minute advice to me driving down the ridge, "Jackie, be respective of other people but keep your distance and don't get caught up with their doings!" I'm not sure what that meant, but I had a pretty good idea. After we had checked into the Noel with our bus load of Sumner County recruits, five black guys that I had just met and I headed for the New Era Club on then all black, Jefferson Street in west Nashville. It was packed with about 50 to 60 people, and I was the only white person in the club. Drinks were brought for all of us, and I was treated loyal when they knew we were on the way to war. This was the beginning of many Afro-American friendships. It was the first time I had flown, but I acted with confidence and like I was a seasoned traveler. Most of the guys were not right out of high school nor had any college, so I guess I was worldly!

When we arrived at Ft. Jackson it was 110 degrees if it was 90. We all went through the normal processing of all raw recruits' experiences. Getting up before dawn and running 5 miles before chow didn't really bother me. I was skinny and in good shape. The "wash tub size" steel helmet on my bald head and Dumbo ears made me look like Gomer Pyle. I felt sorry for the fat boys who couldn't tolerate the heat or the long runs. The drill sergeants (DS) were not relentless with their scorn and ridicule. It quickly registered with me what my older brothers preached. As my dear friend Kay from Memphis used to say, "Keep your chin up, your mouth shut, your legs crossed, and go home in a crowd."

We were not allowed to telephone home for several days… It was probably in the second week of torture, and while I was coping, it was inferno hot with all the gear that we had to carry. After noon on a 100-plus day, we were ordered to fall out. "Smokeum," if you were "gotten," the drill sergeant (DS) barked. A bunch of guys, weary and exhausted, were trying to find a hint of a breeze outside our barracks. Soon, here came the DS, and we were terrified that we were in trouble relaxing. "Any of you "dickheads" know how to type?" he barked. It being ingrained in me by the brothers, I kept quiet. I had been instructed by the "masters" that the most appealing request from the DS really meant kitchen police, scrubbing urinals, picking up cigarette butts, or God knows what else. He repeats the request a couple more times with a more insulting tone. I'm thinking to my sweaty self silently that typing in an office, air conditioned, sitting at a desk. I'm not budging. I'm sure that my files had totally been scrutinized as he finally zeroed in on me. "PAYNE, can you type?" I had been a whiz in Ms. Green's typing class, averaging around 40 words a minute. That was exceptionally good. "HOW FAST CAN YOU TYPE, you pig slop diseased ameba?" I had to think that I was impressed he knew that word and if he knew the meaning. "About 60 to 70 words a minute, Sergeant." I mealy replied. "GET YOUR SCRAWNY ASS to your barracks, change your fatigues, polish your boots, and report to the Headquarters office in 30 minutes to report to the Colonel." Had he said, report to the President, report to the Pope, it could not have been any more terrifying. The highest rank we had been around was Captains, and we had to salute the 1st and 2nd Lieutenants like they were Generals. Recruits are terrified of officers. Knowing, I had stepped in a bucket of shit, I complied and the orders and went to the office. I shall never forget the moment. I was nervous, couldn't find my voice, and wanted to be anywhere else than there. I went into the Colonel's office and made a half-ass attempt to report. "PPPPPRIIIIVVVAATTE PAYNE repppporting SIR!" I shall never forget the moment. "Have a seat, Private Payne. Would you like a cigarette? What is your first name?" "Jaaaaaaaaaaaaack." I finally got out! "Where are you from, Jack?" "Portland, Tennessee." I meekly replied. "I am also from Tennessee. I don't remember the city, but it was possibly Lebanon. Do you know Mr. Watt Hardison?" I begin to relax. "Yes, we are neighbors. His farm adjoins ours." It seemed Mr. Hardison, and he had served together in the State Legislation in Nashville in the mid to late 40ies. They also had served together as delegates to the DNC convention in Chicago in 1948. Now, I'm smoking, totally relaxed, and liking this new celebrity status. The Colonel then got down to business. "Pvt Payne, my company clerk, has had to leave on an emergency leave and I cannot get a replacement for him until next week. I need someone immediately. I see you can type, have a couple of years of higher education, and have a clean record. You will be relieved of KP duty, and not have to drill with the battalion. You will have a mess hall pass to go to the front of the line. The only requirement to pass basic training is you must qualify for weapons training. I can have my staff help you with that. Would you be interested in doing this?" I thought I had died and gone to heaven. My reputation among my buddies went up immensely. I answered the telephone, did filing, and did some typing. The Colonel never called me Jack again or offered me a cigarette, plus everybody around him, including me, was terrified of him. When I finally got to phone home, I was the acting company clerk! My brothers never totally believed me, but from that act of God, I got to go Ft. Ben Harrison Post in Indianapolis, IND, to attend the Adjacent General School for future training, and it aligned me for duty in Germany and escape Vietnam for the rest of my tour of duty.

Ft. Ben Harrison was like being in college. We wore civilian clothing. We lived in barracks that were more like hotels than billets. The ratio was 50-50 with females to males. We ate together and had a full range of the post. All weekends were free, and normally, I rotated between going to Louisville or Nashville. I could fly to Nashville for something like fifteen or twenty dollars. Hitchhiking was very safe, and it was less than $100 to Louisville. Fred and Mayme normally drove me back to the post on Sunday afternoons. One standout memory, they took me to the 1880 Club. It was an old mansion on 4th Street that had been converted into a posh restaurant and nightclub. Sara Keeney was appearing. Sara was friends with Fred. She had been friends with my brother Harold through music, and I met her for the first time at Harold's funeral. I was then 17. Anyway, for some strange reason, I had on my uniform. Sara was a commutate performer and could command the room. Anyway, during her set, she acknowledged Fred and Mame for being there, and then the spotlight shone on me. She mentioned Harold and how her baby brother had grown up and served his country and came over and sang to me, sequined gown, spotlight, and all. The song was "More" from Monte Conte.

From Ft. Ben Harrison in the fall of 1964 led me to Ft. Dix to process to Europe. Ft Dix was cold and dirty and my first realization of army life since Ft. Jackson. My billet was at cross streets of Nashville and Tennessee. Go figure. The post did allow me to meet new friends and was close to New York City. I received an order for Europe about a week before Labor Day. I had been home shortly before Ft. Dix orders, but Dad thought it a good idea to come home one last time before going overseas. Labor Day morning I was at LaGuardia at 5 for a 6 AM flight. I noticed a gaudy, disheveled, dark glasses-blonde bombshell in a fur coat that flirted with me while boarding. I was in my uniform and must say, looked sharp. The plane was nearly empty, and we both had rear seats across from each other. There might have been another exchange of words, but she was asleep before the plane taxied down the tarmac. That afternoon on TV, with a live cut to Nashville, Jane Mansfield in a low-cut gown came out looking like a goddess on the Jerry Lewis Telethon. I regret that I didn't get her autograph or at least engage in more conversation.

It seemed the Ft. Dix days lasted forever. The reason of course, the priority was Vietnam and every plane; every available ship was going west and not east. Thanksgiving was here and the folks didn't push me to come home so soon after Labor Day.

I had met a new friend who was from New York City. Danny also was awaiting orders and I think he might have been in the Adjutant General Judicial Corp. He was cultured and from a Wall Street banking family, obviously raised with cloth napkins and didn't need to be at Ft. Dix. Danny invited six or so guys to come to the City for Thanksgiving. It was my first time in New York, and I tried, as usual, to be cool. I had never ridden a subway before or seen tall buildings. I didn't know what to expect and after a night of bar hopping, Danny finally took us home. All seven of us. The home was on the far East side near Central Park and a brownstone as big as a hotel. Ringing the bell at probably 3 AM, his father came to the door and acted mad that he was going to get a gun, call the police, and how dare he (Danny) bring home half the post. He then broke into a burst of hysterical laughter, and it was just a ruse to get Danny's goat. There seemed to be several bedrooms, and his nymphomaniac sister quickly cabbaged on to Rutherford, a 6-foot-6 football player from KY, to take to her room to shack up with. I finally got to bed, and the next morning, I heard screaming and hollowing and banging on all the doors. Whiskey Sours in the den in fifteen minutes. GET UP. It was Danny's Mom who was already on her way to being crocked at 9 AM. I hadn't ever seen so much opulence. There were at least three cooks and a butler or two. Dinner went well; I was seated next to a Dutch ambassador's wife who couldn't speak English. Danny's Dad was intrigued by my southern accent, and of course, being me, I laid it on thick. After dinner, he, in a velvet smoking jacket with an ascot, said, "Jackson, let's retire to the library for a brandy." Sheepishly, I followed him into a room where the table was as big as our living room. Leather-bound books on the wall and a large gold French telephone on the table where he sat. "Oh, Jackson, what are the folks doing down in Tennessee?" "Oh, Sur, probably having a hont (hunt)." "A what?" he said? "A fox hont!" "Well, Jackson," picking up the phone, "let's give them a call and say hello to them for Thanksgiving." "Oh no, sir, the staff is all off for the holidays. Granny's got rheumatism from drinking so many mint juleps, and it's not a good time. If they aren't having a hont, they will be at The Club." Pressing me for the number, I slowly cited it but prayed that no one would answer. Damn it, Mom answered on the second ring. Hi Mawmaw! (she) WHAT? Mawmaw! (she) Jackie, are you drunk? No Mawmaw. (she) What is this Mawmaw shit? Are you having a hont? (she) WHAT? A hont! WE ARE KILLING HOGS! Ah, how delightful. Who's there? (she) The Parties, the Hudson, etc. Well, ta ta! Danny's Dad did not "out or embarrass me," but he being a brilliant professional person, I am sure, saw through my feeble act. As I have matured, I have tried to be less pretentious but I still like to mingle the upper classes. It's clear that I had probably seen a stage production of Auntie Mame! I told this story to my Mom just a few years before she passed, and she loved it and used it in my face to embarrass me when she thought I was trying to put it on air! She was more attuned to me than I gave her credit. How amazing this story would have been for the Wall Street Banker if I had initially told him the truth, been myself, about butchering our own hogs and a working cattle and horse farm sans Whiskey Sours.

It was a cold, foggy, and drizzling rainy day in November when we sailed out of the Port of Authority on the USS Darby. The destroyer ship was on loan from the US Navy to transport Army troops to Bremerhaven, Germany, to be deployed all over Europe. The climate weather did not stop me from going top side to get a panorama view of the New York skyline and see The Stature Liberty goodbye. Ms. Liberty looked very majestic on Bledsoe Island as we passed. The cruise was somewhat choppy sailing. We took the northern passage route, and most days, it was too raw to go topside. I was able to get a job in one of the many offices to occupy my time and was too busy to get seasick. The trip took about 5 to 6 days. Many of the guys did get sick and had a miserable crossing. The crew kept us informed of where we were. I went up to see the white cliffs of Dover about 3 o'clock in the morning the day before we docked. It was an awesome sight to see the cliffs in darkness, with nothing but the moonlight to illuminate them. Also, at one point, when in the English Channel, we could see both England and France. It made me realize how small the planet is. As we were nearing the shore, we could see the large ESSO fuel storage tank with "Welcome to Germany" blazed on the side. When I disembarked from the ship, I was in Bremerhaven, Germany. I have said before that my year in Germany was one of the most rewarding experiences of my life. I left a boy and returned a man. It not only matured me but also allowed me to travel extensively all over Europe, gain an education that I never would have gotten in school, and make lifelong friendships that I shall treasure for the rest of my life. With my AG schooling in Indianapolis, I was able to get a good job. I was a company clerk for the 114 Supply and Service Battalion at Spinelli barracks in Ludwigshafen, a suburb of Mannheim. I was assigned to Headquarters Company and had a free run of the base. Working for the Colonel meant I had access to a jeep to run errands for him. He also had his own personal driver. I was exempt from KP and other duties required of the soldiers. I was in an office with a Master Sergeant, and he was my immediate superior. Sgt. Harrington was a career soldier from Belfast, Ireland. His wife Marie was French, and they had two or three children. Sgt. Harrington liked me because he had been stationed in states at one point and loved Southerners. He always had my back, and we would frequently go to dinner at a local Gesthaus for "rump steak." He was fluent in Deutch and I learned much from him. Beneath the Colonel at work was a Captain to whom the Sgt. had to report. The captain had to receive all correspondence first to approve it before it would be sent to the Colonel. I hated the Captain, and he hated me. Many times, we would end in a shouting match, and he would circle with a red pen anything he felt was wrong. He would bring it back to either me or the Sgt. and throw papers on my desk and scream, "don't they have schools in Tennessee!) He was insecure, a bald little man with a squeaky voice and whose wife was screwing half the base. The straw that broke the camel's back, I had labored over a long letter that the Colonel needed promptly. The Sgt. okayed it and took it in to be okayed by the Captain. I had changed the word he had written to type regardless to regardless. The Sgt agreed I was correct. After he got the letter, the Captain saw the correction and tore into my office with the letter and had the word circled in red pencil. I was livid. I had pent-up frustrations with him for months. I was letting them all out. The Sgt is trying to hush me, but I'm screaming louder, and he is screaming, saying I'm going to be court-martialed, lose my job, be canned. Who walks through the door but the Colonel? The Sgt explained the whole saga to him, and to my surprise, the Colonel took up for me and reprimanded the Captain right there. He tried everything in the book to get me demoted. I had just designed the battalion crest; the Colonel liked it, and I was promoted to Sp4 class. I visited about 10 countries while being stationed in Germany. Paris was one of my first trips to see Europe for the first time. Daddy was stationed there during the liberation in World War One, and I had overheard stories about the left bank and the art colonies. Mother had also heard because she was eager to offer me advice, "Don't go near Pig Alley"? I seriously thought it might also be some sort of an animal stockyard. Little did I know that it was just a human stockyard!

Please refer to Chapter 16, Chapter Travel, to get a more vivid account of my first visit to the "City of Light."

PFC Jackie D. Payne Wins Battalion Contest For Slogan And Crest

MANNHEIM, GERMANY (AHT-NC)—Thanks to efforts of PFC Jackie D. Payne, (above), son of Mr. and Mrs. George W. Payne, Portland, Tenn., the 115th Supply and Service Battalion here has a crest and slogan. Payne created them himself and won the battalion contest for the slogan and crest that best represented the mission of the 115th.

Payne chose "strength in support" as the motto because the 115th is the supply and service battalion serving all of the Seventh Army.

The motto is in black letters within a yellow stripe running diagonally from the bottom center to the top center of the crest. The crest itself is blue and rimmed wih silver.

Payne received a certificate of achievement for his efforts and a $25 savings bond.

The 22 year old soldier entered the Army in June 1964 and completed basic training at Fort Jackson, S. C.

He attended the University of Tennessee.

PFC Jackie D. Payne

Chapter Six: JDWP

I sign my artwork JDWP. This stems from sage advice from Ms. Wallace, an eccentric maiden, Scottish art teacher at Western Kentucky University. I can still hear her thick brogue, "Don't gild the lily." She meant I don't "overpaint" the artwork with too much. It was she who prompted me to purchase an original Marc Chagall pen and ink. Always sign your finished artwork; be proud to claim it. If you get criticism, claim it anyway and perfect it, was her mantra. Choose a name that you can relate to. A name that people see can be identified when they see other works bearing that signage. Always sign your work.

Good advice. Thus: JDWP

My Christian name at birth was Jackie Donald Payne, or at least that is what is on my birth certificate. Why I was not named John and not the diminutive, I shall never now. Although popular, there were famous celebrities: Jackie Gleason, Jackie Chan, Jackie Cooper and Jackie Mason. I, from an early age, preferred to be called Jack. My sister Anna detested it when she was called ANNER! I even went through a period at school when I signed my homework, Jacky. Now, that frustrated the teachers. My step-grandfather, John Andrew Payne, lived with the family. He shot himself in the throat in our living room stairwell just a few days before I was born. Mom was napping on a day bed in the dining room. She heard the rifle shot, knowing what had just happened, and quietly slipped out the back door to begin ringing the dinner bell. A large crowd soon gathered. John Mitchell Payne, my step-cousin who lived next door, was named for my stepfather. There was not a great deal of love lost between my Mom and John A., so I can rationale why I was not named after him. Years later, Mom shared with me that I was almost named Kenneth...now where that came from, I shall never know.

My father's birth name was George Washington Witham. When he was three or four, my grandmother Laura Veteto divorced my grandfather Sherman Witham and married John Payne. Dad was never legally adopted, and his name was undocumented and changed to Payne. There was much animosity and ill will between the Witham family from the Veteto family. Dad was denied knowing his biological family until he was married with children. It was not until several years later he connected with his brother Fred. Fred was in Portland from Memphis to pick strawberries and met and dated a neighbor girl and family friend, Catherine Crafton. The Craftons and the Paynes were friends and neighbors. Fred knew he had an older brother who bore the name Payne. That union led to many years of Dad getting to know and love his siblings. Much legal confusion lay in store years later for Dad, and he had to have his name legally changed to George Washington Witham Payne.

Dad knew little about his father and ancestors. Attempts by my sister to connect the KY Withams' never came to fruition. After retiring and returning from Atlanta, I researched and connected with them. Sadly, Dad never knew his large family and the strong Methodist, not catholic, Christian and work ethics they fully possessed.

I am proud of my Witham ancestry, and to honor that, I added a "W" to my art signage.

Glenn Witham, a pharmacist, owned the Consumer Drug store in Portland. He was from KY and married a local girl, Donna Green. He had dark eyes and hair, an outgoing personality, and was very approachable. These are traits of the Witham family. Ann frequented Consumers and shared Dad's story with Glenn. He told Ann his ancestors were from the Clinton and Cumberland Counties near Wolf Creek Dam on the Cumberland River. Nearby towns are Jamestown and Russell Springs, Kentucky. Years later, I found on a written note that Ann had jotted. My sister-in-law, Mayme Nelson, married my brother, Fred, who was from Russell Springs, and attested that Witham was in the counties.

Glenn promised to get his oldest relative's address for Ann to contact and try to share a connection. Sadly, Glen suddenly passed, and Ann's health deteriorated, preventing her from seeking out any ties. Progress lay dormant. Glenn and Donna had three children who were near the same age and friends with Laura and Lanna and went to school together in Portland. After Glenn's death, Donna and children relocated to Florida. Lanna was visiting my house one afternoon and received a photo and text from Mark, Glenn's oldest son. It was a honeymoon photo taken of him and his new wife on a cruise ship. I had never met Mark. Looking at the photo, it was chilling the resemblance to our kin. I got his email address and sent him a very detailed account. Could I possibly connect with him? He was very forgiving and said I needed to contact his aunt, Mable Bledsoe, Glenn's older sister in Columbia, KY. I called Mabel and told her the full story. It was like I had known her for years. She wanted to know how soon I could visit her. I made the trek the next day. Even though she had health limitations, she had a bountiful meal and was gracious with information. She said you must meet Uncle Wendall. I couldn't wait.

Wendell was my 2nd cousin. He was 89 years old when we met. He still had twinkling eyes, still drove a vehicle, and put out a garden. His father, Thomas Joshua, was a brother to my grandfather, Sherman Witham. We drove to Wendell's house. It sat back off the main road on Witham Road. It was still a beautiful old white two-story Victorian with gingerbread trimming. He could not have been more gracious to me. He showed us the house, taking us upstairs, where there were many large portraits in gilded frames. He found the family bible. I opened it to the center, and there, my grandfather, George Sherman Witham, displayed with birth and death with listings of his parents and siblings. I feel a sense of pride and remorse that Dad could not have been with me. It was the closest moment I have had to my ancestral past. To date, I still correspond with distant cousins Becky in San Diego, cousins Jackie in Minnesota, and Gene in Albany, KY. Sadly, we lost Mabel Bledsoe of Columbia, KY, but I tried to attend the annual Witham reunion at Wolf Creek Dam in KY.

Jack Payne

Jack Payne can trace his art talents back to his first box of crayons at age three. He later honed his skills while daydreaming in the classrooms of Portland, TN, Elementary and High Schools… drawing houses, Indians, or anything else that came to mind. He was perennially selected to do the holiday scenes in color on the classroom chalk boards.

Jack is passionate about *plein air* painting and can be seen for long hours with brushes in hand on his Old Hickory Lake boat dock. He is a world traveler and always takes photos for later reference in his paintings. Jack has been a professional photographer for 40+ years and has retired from all of the following: Bel Air Studios, Keepsake Portraits, World Portraits, and American Airlines.

Payne considers himself largely self-taught, despite having majored in art at Western Kentucky University. He has also studied with Charles Brindley. He refers to his style as "Grandpa Moses," describing his artwork as semi-realist, near-primitive, using bold color, and not always adhering to dimension and form.

Memberships:

- Monthaven Art Society, Hendersonville
- Ray Cash Memorial American Legion, past Commander
- Professional Photographers of America, former member
- Nashville Chamber of Commerce, former member
- Master Gardeners of Sumner County

He signs his artwork, "JDWP" for Jack Donald Witham Payne.

You may contact Jack Payne at his residence:

Maui Manner

195 Indian Lake Apr 2428, Hendersonville, TN 37075

615-826-5914

jpayne9488@att.net

Alte Bruche & Schloss, Heidelberg, Germany

L&N Train Depot, Portland, TN

806 Piedmont, Atlanta, GA

Payne Farm, Portland, TN

Chapter Seven: Neighbors /Austin Community

I grew up in the Austin community about five miles west of Portland. The "Ole Brick", built circa the early 1800s, located across the Austin Branch and still sits high on a hill from my Grandparents, Albert and Lillie Johns, farm. It changed hands several times over the years. In the 1910 era, it was owned by the Chennault family. They operated a summer school, similar to a Montorosri or finishing school. My mother attended as a young girl. She was taught cooking, manners, and how to sew. All the proper things a young lady needed to know. It was in the garden that she and Dad exchanged wedding vows July 2, 1922, by Rev G. Austin. The original plantation was several hundred acres. Our family farm, now owned by my nephew Dr. Tom and Kelly Short, was originally part of the land grant. Austin school was built on the site where now my late brother Bob's house stands. The land was donated by the Austin family to erect a school with the stipulation; the land would revert to current owners when not operated as a school. The First Baptist Church of Portland was chartered at the school. My grandmother and most of my aunts and uncles joined, and it remains our home church; both my parents attended the original Austin school. A new school was built in 1931, directly across the street from my home. It ceased being a school in 1949-50 and reverted to Ernest Pirtle. I started to Portland Elementary in 1949. My first-grade teacher was Ms. Sally McNeil. Miss Willie Corkran was a revered teacher at Austin. She was a sister-in-law to my mother's sister, Velma Johns Corkran. She not only taught my mother at Austin, but she also later taught most of my siblings. She had a quiet demeanor and went to Macon, Georgia, to attend Wesleyan College at the early turn of century of 1900s. I have fond memories of her. She never married. Her father, William, was an educator and was known as Professor Corkran. The Corkran family lived on Buntin Mill Road between Grandmas farm and Rollie and Elsie Searcy home. They were a large family. Willie, Lee, Mary and Edith never married. Like Willie, Mary, and Edith taught school. Julius was one of the middle sons and married Velma Johns. Velma was my mother's older sister. Years later, my cousin Daniel purchased the family farm, and he would frequently spend weeks there when he had time off from Eastern Airlines. I have fond memories of visiting Dan and he was an inspiration to seek employment for an airline.

The Pirtle family was more than neighbors. Mom and Ernest (Mutt) Pirtle were distant cousins. My great grandmother was Margaret (Pirkle) Pirtle. My Dad and Mr. Ernest were best friends and grew up together. That bond lasted 60 years, and at my father's wake, Mr. Ernest, came up to me at the casket. He had tears in his eyes and said he had lost his best friend. I treasure that moment because, like best friends, Dad and he would have petty differences, and the next moment, Mr. Ernest would be visiting. Ms. Emma was a class act. I remember her as being quiet in nature. She and Mom would have quilting parties at each other's house. The friendship extended to their children with my siblings. There were five in the Pirtle clan. Their ages were near to my brothers and sister. Arnold and J.T. had already gone from home. Margaret and Loree were like sisters to Ann. Jerry (Shine), the youngest child, was the best friend and partner in crime to my brother Fred. Jerry, in high school, dated my first cousin, Ruth Scott. Years later, both widowed, they met, dated and married and shared several blissful years together. I had a delightful visit with Arnold Pirtle Aug 23,2018. Note: (Since I have written this account, we lost Arnold, April 2024). He is buried in Chicago, Illinois, with his beloved Barbara.) He now lives in Stevensville, MT, with his son Ralph. He is the last of the "old guard" neighbors of our Austin community. He is the spitting image of Mr. Ernest, his father, and possesses much of his class. He enlightened me the day my step grandfather, John Andrew (JA) Payne committed suicide. He and James Hudson) were the first on the scene from my mother ringing the dinner bell (we had no phone), and they both raced to Grandmas to call Mr. Deaux, the magistrate for the community and Wilkinson Wiseman Funeral Home.

Another enduring family that was next door neighbors were the Hudson family. Their farm was directly across Riggs Road from Tom and Kellys home. It is now owned by the David Ammotte family. Note: (This account, David passed in early 2024.). One lasting memory from my youth was killing hogs on Thanksgiving Day over a period of years at their farm. One memory that stands out from those years was Mr. Hudson's death in 1949, being found in the outhouse privy. He was "laid out" in the front parlor, the first experience I had with death and the three daughters, Marjorie, Anna Belle, and Eva Nell, doting on my cuteness! I was nearly 6 years old. Another year, the Carter farm mansion fire made the news. Still another year, Hank Williams dying on New Year's Eve. We, perhaps were killing hog again at the Hudson farm. Even more eerie recall, brother Harold, a young teen, saying out of the blue at the breakfast table, I dreamt Mr. Tom Jones passed last night. Tom and Mayme, and their son David lived on the left of Gallatin Road, going toward Hwy 52. There was silence, and a few minutes later, another neighbor showed and said, Mr. Jones passed last night (1949). Harold had no way to have known that he had died, and Mr. Jones was not critical. My brother Bob was killed in a traffic accident on what we call The Jones hill. There always seemed to be an epic event to record history. James was the Hudson's only son and a workhorse. He worked the Hudson farm and always had the best crops. He had a brief marriage to Edith Short, my brother-in-law Tom's older sister. James married later in life after Miss Minnie passed and moved to Gallatin, remarried and raised a family. Rollie (Searcy) was cousins to Hattie Mae, Ann's best friend, and Elsie was always fun to be around. She had a tremendous sense of humor and was very candid. I loved visiting them, and they would come to our house nearly every Saturday night in the wintertime to watch television and play rook. Mom always had plenty of homemade tomato juice, and Dad a crackling fire in the fireplace. Harvey and Lucille Groves lived on the left before Crafton Road. Their son Glen was my age and my best friend in the early years. The Harpers were a large family of eight. My step Grandfather was John Payne, and his sister Myra married Marshall Green Harper. They had seven sons who grew up with my father, George Witham Payne. They were very close in age and bonded as cousins. The Shorts lived across the Red River, first farm on the right. Just like the Pirtles and Hudson, they were near the same age of my siblings. There were seven children like our family, and who would have predicted their youngest son, Thomas C., would wed my sister Anna Elizabeth Payne?

Austin community was idyllic in the 50ies. Neighbors shared joys and sorrows with each other. They were like family. They didn't lock your doors at night. I shall expound on more neighbors in later chapters.

It's uncanny, with the passing of Arnold, I am the last of the old guard of Austin Community.

Jack In Rock Garden on Home Farm

Colonel or Thresher and Fifi

Two of the family dogs through the years

Chapter Eight: Family

Laura Tabitha Veteto and George Sherman Witham married in Wilson Co., TN, in Sept 1894. Their only child was George Washington Witham Payne born in June 1895. He was called G.W. his entire life. He was named for his grandfather, whom he never knew, George Washington Witham of KY. They divorced and Laura then married John Andrew Payne in July 1898. George was three years old. He was called George Payne until he registered for Social Security and had to have his name made legal. He chose George Washington Witham Payne. Here is a synopsis of my ancestors.

PAYNE

The name Payne is part of the ancient legacy of the early Norman inhabitants that arrived in England after the Norman Conquest in 1066. Payne was a Norman name used for a person who lives in the country or a person whose religious beliefs are somewhat suspect. Checking further, we found that was derived from the Old English word paien, which was derived from the latin word pagsnus, meaning rustic or countryman. Early records of the name Payne in the Chronicles of England show that the ancestors of the bearers of this name were of the Norman race. I trace the Payne lineage ten Generations: Thomas Payne, 1657 Petworth, Sussex, England, Middle Temple Barrister Marr to Margaret Wheatley, Yorkshire, England. John A. Payne (1870-1943), my stepfather. He shot himself in the stairwell of our home approximately 2 weeks before I was born. My mother was resting in the bedroom and heard the shots. He was oldest of nine children born to Marion Mitchell 1851- 1923 (TN) and Elizabeth Jane Boston 1852-1926 (TN).

WITHAM

This is a copy of Becky Bucalo's account of Witham research. {After years of research by family members, we have learned that the first direct ancestor to come to America was Peter Witham. He was born in 1627 in Steeple, Essex, England. He came to America via the ship Abigal by way of Canada to Boston, Mass, where he married Redigon Clark June 17th, 1652. They settled in Kittery, York, Maine. Most of their approximately 11 children were born in Boston, Mass or Kittery, Maine. Peter had a second wife, Eunice. I wanted to establish this history prior to proceeding. Let it be known, throughout history the spelling of Witham has taken on many spellings. Some are misspellings and evolved spellings. Ie: Wittum, Whithum, Whitham, Wytham. We identify our direct ancestor as Witham.

Fast forward approximately 5 generations later, the Witham's apparently migrate to Virginia and then to Saline, Arkansas. Some of that generation stayed in Saline, and others migrated to Kentucky. Which brings us to the most well-known couple George Washington Witham, b 1831-1906 and his wife Catherine Bunch Witham, b 1832-1922. Many accounts from state that our Catherine Bunch Witham was of Native American decent, Cherokee reportedly. Although these accounts cannot be proven on paper, research has shown that quite possibly, she descended from the Melungeon people. This research has shown one very common surname for the Melungeon people, is "Bunch." This research is a work in progress. The Witham's are a proud, hardworking, independent, bull headed "Bunch." Pun intended. Thanks to Becky for this account.

The Witham family that I have a record that goes back to Witham (Essex), England. It dates to the Roman empire and was a main route. It has a population of about 60,000 people, or, the size of Hendersonville. It is on the train line about 38 miles north of London. The first account of is Peter Witham.

VETETO

The Vetetos were originally French and were Huguenots. Records indicate the Dutch Reform Church of New Netherlands (NYC) as such. 1749, Jeremiah Veteto is listed as paying taxes in Virginia. The farthest I can trace is that his son, Stephen, fought for

Virginia in the Revolutionary War. In 1749, Jeremiah Veteto is listed as paying taxes in Virginia. The names of his children may have been Samuel, Daniel, Stephen, Jeremiah. There is a mystery to me, my grandmother, Elizabeth Richerson of Granville, TN, in Jackson County. She was married to William Veteto, and he is buried single in Maple Hill Cemetery in Portland, TN. I can't find a trace of a marriage bond or divorce record or any indication they were married. She was killed in a tornado stripping tobacco. She is buried in an unmarked grave at the Red River Meeting House in the Presbyterian Church of Schochoh, KY, near Adairville, in Logan Co. in KY.

PERDUE

As per Lee Alton Absher, MD. [According to the manuscript. "Descendants of Dr. Willaim Perdue" by Robert Hartley Perdue, the name Perdue is Norman in Origin. The tradition is that the early Perdues were Huguenots, and they left France and Ireland before coming to America. It is not known who the first Perdue was to come to America. Dr. William Perdue came to Pennsylvania from County Antrim, Ireland, in April 1737. The Latin name is Perdeum, meaning God's Help. William Perdue is the first family we have a record of. He lived from about 1550 to 1620 in Winchester, England. The Perdues were prominent bell founders in England and Ireland. Bells in many English and Irish cathedrals were cast by them.]

MARLIN

Archibald Martin Marlin was born October 24, 1757, died in 1830. He was married to Martha Ferrier April 11, 1780, and died after 1830 in Sumner Co., TN. He is buried in the old Nashville cemetery on 4th Street North. He is my 6th generation. He is my grandfather.

My grandmother was Lillie Marlin Johns. Her mother was Sarah Ann Elizabeth Perdue. Her mother was Harriet Wyatt (1813-1888) and, second wife, and one of 14 children born to Daniel Perdue (1786-1857). Her father was a very rich man, owning more than 100 slaves, a mill and distillery. He was an early pioneer of Sumner

County. His father was Meshack Perdue (1756-1838), VA and a wealthy landowner in Virginia. He owned three slaves in 1820.

PIRKLE/PIRTLE

The following is a direct quote from my 3rd cousin on Verline (Moms) side. Kathy Little's son, Travis Little, pastor of 1st Baptist Church, Silver Point, TN. who, shared Jerry Pirtle, as grandfather-in-law. Jerry was a distant cousin. [The Pirtle/Pirkle family has a rich and diverse history spanning generations. Originating in Europe, the family migrated to the United States, settling primarily in the Southern states. The Pirtle/Pirkles were known for their strong family values, resilience, and determination. They established themselves as farmers, business owners, and community leaders, leaving a lasting impact on their communities.]

Travis also added: Margaret Mitchell, in her epic novel, (Gone with the wind), wrote that "The Wilkes and the Hamilton's always marry their cousins. And while we might not consider cousins as appropriate sweethearts here in the New South, it was indeed a very common practice during the nineteenth century, a practice the Pirtle and the Pirkle branches of my mother's family tree turned into an art. Arriving in Pennsylvania prior to the American Revolution between the years of 1731 and 1734. Hans Jacob Berkle and his wife Dorotha, would go on and have some eleven children. Historical records indicate that after arriving in the Americas, Hans changed the family surname to Purkle. Over the years that followed, due to the intensive amount of intermarrying, the surname went on to include Pirtle, Purkle and Purtle.

Of their surviving children, many of the males made their way to Rockingham, North Carolina, prior to or shortly after the American Revolution. This includes John Jacob Pirtle Sr. Following the resolution, the Pirtles joined countless others pursuing American Westward Expansion. This led to some of the Pirtles going to Hall County, Georgia, and White County, Tennessee, as my ancestors did. Even though they were separated by large distances the

Pirtle/Purkles/Purtle still continued to intermarry so much that my mother's tree has three branches that all lead back to Hans Jacob Berkle. It is these intermarriages and this colorful history that has today shaped my background of my family}. Note. As a member of the "Man of the Cloth," I appreciate Travis for an insightful but truthful account of the family. As we have often joked, "I am surprised that we don't have pointed ears.

JOHNS

My grandmother and mother of Albert King Johns (1874-1920) was Margaret Pirtle (1850-1875). She was the daughter of Alexander Pirkle. Margaret was married to James Elias Johns (1847-1924). Albert King Johns (1874-1920) was married to Lillie Mary Marlin (1859-1957) April 10,1896. They had eight children: (1) Margaret Eleanor, (2) James William, (3) Sarah Velma, (4) Verline Ruth, (5) Myrtle Elizabeth, (6) Leonard King (Boy), (7) Emmitt Evans, (8) Lillie Berley.

1. **Margaret Eleanor** (1897-1952) marr to James Jefferson Veteto (1889-1974).
   NOTE: James Jefferson was my grandmother, Laura Tabitha Veteto's younger brother.
   Five children: William King, Gladys Lorene, Edna Maizell, Lillie Elizabeth, James Albert
   - **William King** (1920-1985) marr to Effie Azalee Honeycutt (1924-1983).
     Three children: Jesse D. Sanders, Faye Lee, and Wanda
     J.D. marr Glenda Pearson (divorced)
     One child Jimmy Veteto Sanders (1964) marr to Holly
     J.D. marr Betty
     One child Ryan Sanders (1965)
     Jimmy marr to Holly
     Faye Lee (1946) marr to Jimmy Green (1943-1986)
     Two children: Rita and Ray
     Rita Green (1947) Marr to James Meadors (1950–2021)
     One child: Shaneice
     Jimmy (Ray) William (1965-2018)
     Wanda (1947-2001) marr Jerry Guill
     One Child: Leigh Anne

- **Gladys Lorene** (1923-2023) marr to Harold Vernon Owen (1923-1986).
  Three children: Marvin, Margaret House, and Mary
- **Edna Maizell** (1926-2007) marr to Howard Eugene Carr (1916-?).
  Nine children: Phillip Wayne, Rodney Ray, Norma Jean Hayes, Linda Lee Jennings, Joyce A. Harrod, Karen Lynn Hord, Janet Marie Slanton, Rita Mae Lasko, Tina Marie Allee
- **Lillie Elizabeth** (1929-2013 IND) marr to Herman Joseph Bowe (1928-? IND).
- **James Albert** (1934-1972) marr to Betty Lou Alberhasky (1931-2010).
  Four children:
  Jeffrey Albert (1959 (KY) marr to Lcsa. One child: Allese Reyanne (2002) KY,
  Rebeca Maude (1961 (KY) marr to Michael Joseph Thomas (1955). One child: Brian Patrick (1982).
  Julee Ann (1962) marr to Robert Lee Russell (1962) ILL. Three children: Katthryn Marie (1992), Shannon Nicole (1994), Timothy Albert (1996).
  James Ralph (1965) (KY) marr to Lisa Rene McLennan (1967). Three children: Erin Lea (1997) (KY), Mary Elizabeth (2000) (KY), Matthew (2004) (KY).

2. **James William (Willie)** (1899-1967) marr to Minnie E. Denning (1890-1971). No children.
3. **Sarah Velma** (1902-1982) marr to Julius Trousdale Corkran (1887-1968). Four children: Dorothy Velma, Julius Trousdale, William Albert, Amelia Ann
   - **Dorothy Velma** (1922-1964) marr to Magnus Ezra Phillips. One son: Robert David (1942-2019) OR marr to Sherry Patricia Slade (1946-2021) OR.
   - **Julius Trousdale** (1923-1984) marr to Floraine Delight O'Neil (1926-1992).
     Three children: Julie Lynn, Laura Ann, and Julius Trousdale Daniel
     - **Julie Lynn** (1968) marr to Kenneth Blaine Feeley (1957). No children.
     - **Laura Ann** (1962) marr to Douglas Arthur Leckband (1960).
       One child: Lucas Rhys Douglas (2004).
     - **Julius Trousdale Daniel** (1965) marr to Elizabeth Angela Rocco (1960).
       One child: Gabriel Peter (2007) TN.
   - **William Albert** (1929-2009), CA marr to Janet Miriam Blanchfield (1934-2023) CA.

Five children: Christopher Michael, Steven Daniel, Kelley Anne, Carolyn Patricia, Constance
- **Christopher Michael** (1959) marr to Wendy Ann Whittaker (1965).
- **Steven Daniel** (1964) marr to Dianne Kay Schuman (1964).
- **Kelley Anne** (1962) marr to James Butler (1964) LA.
- **Carolyn** (1963) single.
- **Constance** (1966) marr to Curtis Wayne Costanza (1963).

- **Amelia Ann** (May 9, 1942) CA single.

4. **Verline Ruth** (NOTE: This is my mother, and a detailed genealogy follows in subsequent pages).
5. **Myrtle Elizabeth** (1906-1985) marr to William Atlas Scott (1906-1972). Three daughters: Ethel Katherine, Agnes Gaynell, and Alma Ruth
    - **Ethel Katherine** (1927-2022) marr to J.B. Dorris (1923-2000). Three sons: William Earl, twins: Larry Gene, Gary Dean
        - **William Earl** (1944-2019) marr to Hollice Arlene Huck.
          Two children: Rachel Elise (1973) and Jonathan Scott (1969).
        - (twins): **Gary Dean** (1947) marr to Paula June Dickey (1949).
          Two children: Christopher Dean (1970), Susan Raquel (1967).
        - **Larry Gene** (1947) marr to SueEllen Hayes (divorced).
          Larry Gene marr to Mary Frances Leftner (1944).
    - **Agnes Gaynell** (1926-2014) marr to Orvil Houston Freedle (1919-2008).
      Three children: Nancy Ann, Ralph Houston, and Donna Lynn
        - **Nancy Ann** (1943) marr to Bobby Dean Belt (1942) (divorced).
          Three children: Deborah Denene, Kenneth Dean, Mark Wesley.
        - **Ralph Houston** (1951) marr to Linda Ann Yates (1951).
          Three children: Roderick Houston, Carrie Melin, Matthew Scott.
        - **Donna Lynn** (1954) marr to James Walton Wiggins (1953) (divorced).
          Three children: Margot Coirsdan, Twins: Natalie Olivia, Nathaniel Allen.
    - **Alma Ruth** (1930-2011) marr to T.C. Hudddleston (1921-1971).
      Three children: Glenna Faye Vincent, Danny Ray, and Kathy Gayle Little.

        - **Glenna Faye** (Oct 26, 1948) marr to Jack Vincent (divorced).
          Three children: Terri Rae, Nicole Lynn, Jacquline Faye.
            - **Terri Rae** marr to Douglas Darrow (divorced). Terri Rae marr to Jonathan Freedle (divorced). One child: Norah Freedle.
        - **Danny Ray** (July 11, 1955) marr to Rhonda Sue Tucker (Feb 24, 1957).
          Two children: Lisa Renee (June 29, 1974) and Chad Daniel (May 19, 1979).
            - **Chad Daniel** (May 19, 1979) marr to Alana Clark (Jan 11, 1978).
              Three children: Eli Clark (Mar 1, 2005), Evan Ray (Apr 12, 2007), Emery Danielle (Mar 14, 2009).
            - **Lisa Renee** (June 29, 1974) marr to Jason Kyle Stanton (Aug 3, 1973).
              Three sons: Twins: Tucker Kyle (May 25, 1998), Todd Clay (May 25, 1998), Ty Dawson (Aug 11, 2005).
        - **Kathy Gayle** (Oct 23, 1959) marr to Robert Bruce Little (Nov 24, 1953).
          Three children: Justin Scott, Travis Chase, Katherine Angela Elizabeth (KAEL).
            - **Justin Scott** (Oct 6, 1980) marr to Allison Carol Tignor (Apr 6, 1979).
              Two children: Samantha Ruth (Mar 3, 2010), Wesley Chase (Sep 29, 1984).
            - **Travis Chase** (Sep 29, 1984) marr to Heather Marie Phillips (Oct 26, 1985).
              One child: TC Scott (Jan 19, 2019).
            - **KAEL** (Nov 20, 1985) marr to Justin Jared Hyde (Feb 14, 1986).
              Two children: Addilyn Kate (Nov 16, 2016), Elowen Ramsey Dean (Nov 12, 2018).
        - **Alma Ruth** (1930-2011) marr to Jerry Pirtle (1928-2014).

6. **Leonard King (Boy)** (1908-1988) marr to Blanche Miller (1910-1976). No children.
7. **Emmett Evans** (1910-1979) single.
8. **Lillie Berley** (1914-1997) marr to Willie Gray Scott (1916-1978).
   Nine children: Lilly Florence, Billy Moore, Roy King, Shirley Jo, Peggy Sue, Mary Alice, Jill, Jack, James Gray (Jimmy)
    - **Lilly Florence** (1938) marr to Gerald Duran (divorced).
      One daughter: Stephanie Osment (Feb 21, 1963).

- **Billy Moore** (1941-2018) marr to Patricia Ann Hughes (1947). One daughter: Melissa Jo Hyten (Feb 1, 1967).
- **Roy King** (1942-2015) marr to Agnes Tarrents (1946-?). Three sons: Stephen Roy (1966), Kevin Dewayne (1972), and Travis Earl (1977).
- **Shirley Jo** (1968) marr to James Brown (1941). One daughter: Melanie (1968) marr to Richard Waltz (IL).
- **Peggy Sue** (1946) marr to Hubert Christian (1943). Two children: Jeffrey (1964) marr to Carol Head (1968), and Tommy Russell (Rusty) (1965) marr to Michele Diane Goodwin (1967).
    - **Jeff** and **Carol** had three sons: Michael Scott, Austin Jeffrey, and Dalton Pierce.
        - **Michael** marr to Megan, **Austin** marr to Chelea, **Dalton** marr to Shelby.
    - **Rusty** and **Michele** had two daughters:
        - **Kalie Lynn** marr to Jerry Christopher Johns.
        - **Beth Nicole** marr to Adam Burkhart.
- **Mary Alice** (1948) marr to Pete Spain (1946-?). Three children: William, twins: Jason and Jada. **Mary Alice** marr to Carl Jenkins (no children).
- **Jill** (1951) marr to Lawrence Davis (divorced). They had three children: Brad (1969), Bethany (1973), Laurie (1974). **Jill** marr to Joel Lamberth (no children).
- **Jack** (1951) marr to Reba Taylor. Two children: Brandon (1985), and Sabrina Renae (1979).
- **James (Jimmy)** (1953). **James** marr to Brenda Kirby. Adopted: Tina and Dawn. **James** marr to Susan. Children: Misty, Dustin, Amanda. **James** marr to Gretchen Stall (no children).

If I have left out any names or dates, please know it was not intentional.

Grono Owen was born in 1844 in Macon Co., TN. He was the son of Abner Owen (1813-1850) and Marthia Clanton (1814-unknown). Grono married Lucinda Johns (1847-1935), daughter of John Abner Johns (1812-1892), and Rebecca Pirtle (1820-1888), granddaughter of Thomas and Meary Elender Johns of NC and VA. During the Civil War, Grono joined the Union Army. He was a Pvt with Co A 94th KY Inf. Grono and Lucinda, in the fall of 1892 with their unmarried children and an elderly slave, left Macon County, TN, in a covered wagon, walking most of the way, and settled in the Lake Springs area of Simpson County, KY. Grono died in 1917, and he and Lucinda are both buried in Peden Mill Cemetery, Simpson Co. KY. (Submitted by Helen Aton – great-granddaughter).

Verline Ruth Johns was born February 1904 to Albert King Johns and Lillie Mary Marlin. She is a direct descendant of Archibald Marlin, a Revolutionary soldier, buried in the old Nashville cemetery, making her a candidate for DAR or the daughters of the American Revolution. Much has been written about him, and was an early pioneer of Sumner County.

Verline Johns was fair in complexion and looked like actress Princess Grace Kelly of Monaco. She processed curly light brown hair and had an innocent persona. She was called "turkey" from her early school days and bore the moniker Turk her entire life.

G. W. was nine years older than she. He was tall and dark complexion, had wavy black hair, and flashing brown eyes. She was smitten by the very handsome and older George. They both attended the one room Austin School located on the Payne farm. Austin school was the charter house for the 1st Baptist Church in Portland, and the foundation of the school is located at Bob's house. G.W. served in World War One in France and declared over in 1918. George returned to the family farm after servicing in the Medics Corp. He marched with his battalion on the Champs Elysees with the liberation of Paris. They married in July 1922 in a garden wedding at the Austin House (old brick) in Portland. George and Verline had seven children. There was a twenty-year and one month age gap difference between Ann and Jack. The following are the seven children listed and their children:

(l) Anna Elizabeth Payne
Anna (Ann) Elizabeth - June 25, 1923 – Oct 12, 2001 (TN)
Married to Thomas C. Short - Feb 5, 1927 - Jun 19, 2004 (TN)
They had two children: Kathryn and Dr. Thomas Harold.

(1a) Kathryn (Kathy) - July 9, 1957, married William Thomas Patten, M.D. - Sep 13, 1953

They had two sons: John Thomas and Daniel Carter:

John Thomas - Apr 26, 1986, married Courtney B. Keen - Sep 13, 2021

They had two children:

Anna Bonde - Sep 13, 2021, and Wyatt Thomas - Feb 18, 2023

William Daniel - Apr 26, 1987, married Emily Jane Cole - Apr 2, 1984 (MS)

They have three children:

Carter Jane - Dec 28, 2017, Cole Thomas - Nov 22, 2019, and Kathryn Ivy Patten - July 6, 2021

(2a) Thomas Harold - Oct 19, 1960, married Lori Ann Allen - Mar 30, 1961 (VT) (Divorced)

They had two children: Julia Elizabeth and Brett Thomas:

Julia Elizabeth - Jul 24, 1994, married Steven Tye Polk - Nov 16, 1993 (TX)

They have 4 children:

Ezekiel James - Sep 16, 2019, (triplets) Brody Thomas, Shepherd Allen, Jovie Cate - July 18, 2023 (TX)

Brett Thomas - Dec 11, 1998, married Baleigh Bennett - Jul 30, 2000

They have 1 son:

Baylor Thomas - Aug 9, 2023

Thomas Harold married Kelly Dee Thompson - Oct 25, 1969

They have one daughter:

Olivia Grace - Oct 31, 2003

(2) George Thomas Payne

One child with Juanita Foster (May 10, 1928 – Aug 20, 2018) (IND)

One child: Vickie G. Sheets McCloskey Ford, married to Rick Ford

Two children: Mark McCloskey Jr., Norman (Markie) McCloskey (deceased)

George Thomas (Tom) - Dec 25, 1925 – Jun 20, 2014 (TN) married Wallita Wayzel - (Feb 13, ? - Sep 18, 2015) (CA) (divorced)

They had three sons: Twins: Stacey, Tracey, and Barry Edward

Stacey - Aug 12, 1961, married to Elaine Davis - May 24, 1961 (CA)

They had two children:

Stacey Christine - Dec 12, 1984 (CA) and Kimberly May - Oct 25,

1985 (CA)

Kimberly May married Stephen P. Goodrich (Divorced)

They had two children:

Noah James and Madison May - Sep 18, 2011

Kimberly May married Marc H. Ball

One child: Keanan Grace Ball - Jan 6, 2019

Tracey married Sheryl Black (divorced)

They have three children:

Tracey Marie - Jul 27, 1982, Loren Anthony Payne Black - Aug 7, 1963, Karla Carlita - Feb 7, 1985

Barry Edward - Nov 13, 1967 (single)

George Thomas married Nell Larson of Jasper, TN

(3) Fred Andrew Payne

Fred Andrew Payne - Apr 24, 1929 - Mar 22, 2011 (TN) married Mayme Nelson - Jul 5, 1931 – Dec 3, 2021 (KY)

They have one daughter:

Angela Dawn - Nov 27, 1974 (KY)

Angela Dawn married Scott Hall - Aug 31, 1930 (KY) (divorced)

They have three daughters:

Sophia Hope - May 23, 2004, Sadie Olivia - Jan 20, 2006, Alexandra Audrey Grace - Mar 13, 2007

(4) Sherman Harold Payne - May 11, 1931 – Mar 3, 1960 (TN)

(5) James (Jim) Oliver Payne

James Oliver - Aug 19, 1933 – Jul 22, 2011 (KY) married Marjorie Richards - Apr 17, 1936 (MI) – Jan 9, 1975 (KY)

They had 4 children: Kimberly Ann, Pamela Jamie, James Harold, and Jon Jared:

Kimberly Ann (Kim) - Jul 9, 1957, married Barry Lee Skaggs - Feb 2, 1960 (KY)

They have twin daughters:

Kendra Leigh - Jun 26, 1963 (Engaged) to Stephen Marks, M.D. - May 1, 1995

Jordan Shea - Jun 26, 1963 (divorced)

Pamela Jamie (Pam) - Oct 5, 1962, married David Edward Bevill - Mar 2, 1959 (GA)

They have two sons:

Zachery David - Dec 2, 1984 (GA)
Aaron James - Oct 21, 1985 (GA)
James Harold (Jim) - Apr 17, 1964 (MI) (single)
Jon Jared - Sep 14, 1966, married Pamela Faye McRorie - Feb 13, 1969
They have two children:
Jacob Cole (Jake) - Dec 12, 2002 (GA)
Ashley Elizabeth - Sep 2, 2005 (GA)
James Oliver married Barbara Ann Wilson Epps - Dec 16, 1939 – Jan 7, 2009 (GA)

(6) Bobby Gene (Bob) Payne
Bobby Gene - Jan 15, 1937 - Jan 6, 1995, married Gloria Jean Stone - Aug 25, 1943 - Jul 11, 2002
They had 3 daughters:
Twins: Lanna Jean and Laura Joan, and Leigh Anne
Lanna Jean - Dec 1, 1970, married Cameron Lynn Smith - Mar 25, 1966 (divorced)
They have two children:
Payne William - May 12, 2003
Preston Engel - Jun 29, 2007
Laura Joan - Dec 1, 1970, married Kelly Gene Evans Jr. - Aug 14, 1972 (LA) (divorced)
They have two sons:
Jordan Thomas - Aug 30, 1996
Christopher Michael Payne - Sep 3, 1998
Leigh Anne (Trip) - Apr 4, 1972 (Single)

(7) Jack Donald Payne (Jack)
Jack Donald Witham - May 23, 1943 (single)

All six sons served honorably in the military, and Ann worked for the Us Navy for 3 years at the pentagon in Washington, D.C. Mother and Dad were ever so proud.

G.W. died suddenly August 28, 1970, from a heart attack. He was found at the hand dug water well at the site of Bob's house under construction. The coroner said he did not suffer, and he always said he wanted to die with his boots on. Verline lived twenty more years at the farm. She died Sept 19, 1990. After Dad's death, she continued to carry on the mantle of family standard that she and G. W. had set. All the siblings came home for the holidays and weekends. She was diagnosed with stomach cancer and stayed her last months at home. We took turns staying with her. I would cook whatever meal she wanted and always tried to make her tray decorative with a fresh flower. It was disheartening to see her only eat a couple of bites of something she requested.

I returned home to not the same person that I had been two years prior. I was more focused and certainly more mature. Mom and Dad were both older and in declining health. Against better judgment, I moved back to the farm. I wanted to spend more time with the family and decide where I wanted to do with my life. Dad had sold my red Corvair Chevrolet, and I didn't have a car. He had purchased a new 1965 Bel Air Chevrolet before I had gotten home. That fall of '66, I enrolled at Western KY University. I usually commuted with Mary Sue and Bill Dye, who worked at Kendell in Franklin. She and I would continue to Bowling Green. Sometimes, I would drive Dad's car, and Frank Collins would ride with me.

I took many crash courses at Western and concentrated more on the social aspects of campus life that I didn't peruse at Draughons. I had mostly art classes and hung out with the Western Players theatre group. I met the love of my life, Marceline Winenger. She was from Canada and majoring in theatre. She was a willowy blonde and a dead ringer for Nicole Kidman. She would have married me on the spot, but I knew she had ambitions and could never be tamed. I ran into her several years later in San Francisco, and we had a remarkable weekend. I never professed to be a great lothario; I didn't date very much in High School; but probably the junior and senior proms. I lost my virginity to an older art student at Western. I dated more when I got to Draughons. At Western, I had muscled up, more mature, a veteran and world traveler and had a flashy sports car, a 1968 Firebird. B. S., whom I shall not identify, was my first sexual conquest. She was an art major from Louisville and as wild as a March hare. She stalked me, and it paid off for her. At the age of 22, she seduced me. I still have a pottery piece she made for me for the rite of passage. I saw her years later driving on the Watterson expressway, and she was enroute to the airport to join the Woman's Army Corp. I often wonder what happened to her. You can say I had three loves in my life. All three have shared 9 husbands among them. I'm still unmarried, and I would say I dodged a bullet as I refer to them as: . No names mentioned, but it was an adventure. You didn't know, did you?

Jim and Marge lived in Houghton-Hancock, Michigan. This is as far as one can get in the Upper Peninsula. It is a barren, cold and desolate place with mostly Finnish/ Scandinavian citizens. It has many abandoned deep copper mines. One was just feet from Jim's back door. Jim was in the last years of his Air Force career and was stationed there (thumb area of Michigan) in 1963/64. Retiring back there in 1966, he had an opportunity to purchase a failing car dealership. It was a GMAC Pontiac/Oldsmobile affiliate and the only one for miles. In 1967, in July, Dad decided to visit them. He had not been near an airplane since World War 1. He didn't have a clue how to navigate an airport as massive as O'Hare in Chicago. I prompted him for days that there were several terminals and he had to take a tram or bus to connect flights. As I feared, he struck out on foot to make his connecting flight on a Blue Goose NW "little bird." He made his connection but after being delayed again on his return in the July snow, vowing never to venture that far away again. He didn't think much about the Upper Peninsula. In 1968, Mom and I decided to visit. As a have said, TC was a boiler maker welder and required him to be out of town a great deal. This time landed him in Ohio. Mom had never flown, and she and I flew from Nashville to Columbus, Ohio. I was very proud of her, and she seemed to enjoy the flight once we got to cruising altitude. Thomas C. met us, driving from Toledo, and we drove through the night to UP. The Mackinac Bridge was new, and was quite an experience driving over it. It was foggy, and I guess it was as well as we couldn't see the ominous waters below. It was a good visit, and I purchased a 1968 Firebird coupe. I was attending

Western and moon lighting, working for Fred at Bel Air. What with my GI bill allotment, I was managing well. The copper Industry tanked, and Jim decided he had purchased a lemon. In spite, they remained there until 1969 before moving to Louisville to join Fred and now me. Bob and Tom would later join the company. At one time, we all worked for Bel Air Studios. Life was very good, and the weekends like a fairy tale.

In May 1954, Jim brought Marge to meet the family prior to their getting married in October. He had a coral Oldsmobile convertible. He had told her he came from an "old South Patrician family," had money and attended Vanderbilt. God know what else. What a cultural shock for Marge to see we barely had running water and indoor plumbing. Despite Jim's lies, Marge bonded and fell in love with our family. Her entire life, she professed that our family was her family. I was 11 years old. Marge was beautiful, with black hair and large brown eyes. She was a dead ringer for Farah Pahlavi of Iran. I felt that I had another sister. She was also deathly afraid of frogs. At her death time, she had a large collection of frogs. Mom and Dad were working in the strawberry fields, and Marge was making lunch. She had me go to the garden for an onion for one of her dishes. I found a large toad hopping in the garden. I came back inside with the frog to taunt her. Screaming murder, she ran out of the house and locked herself in the car. She eventually forgave me, and became very close friends for the rest of her life.

Dad fell in love with Marge as well. It was apparent when they married. Mom was going to order an appropriate gift for them. Dad quickly nixed her offering and said they would spring for a more expensive present, offering fine China set rather than pottery. Good for Dad! Mom and Dad were eager to show her off to friends and neighbors. Visiting Ms. Minnie Hudson, a sweet high opinionated neighbor, and her son James were one of the first to go visit. Ms. Minnie, consumed with her beauty and charm, kept repeating over and over, James! "Ain't she pretty."

In 1956, Fred, Mom, Dad, and I visited Marge and Jim in Port Austin, MI. He was stationed in the Air Force and met Marjorie Richards from neighboring Bad Axe. In spite of Fred's pleas to Mom to give the ETA, we arrived earlier than expected. He thought he had another day before the "trooping of the guard" from Mom. We pulled into the driveway, and Jim looked ashen and he had seen a ghost. There were piles of beer cans at least three feet high and oblivious accumulated for several weeks. Mom managed to contain herself. Dad fell in love with Marge's Dad, and they reminisced about World War 1 stories. The same bond applied with Margaret and Verline. We toured the thumb of Michigan and drove into Canada to Sarina and London, Ontario. The border patrol officer zeroed in on Dad. "Where were you born?" Daddy, obviously flustered, replied, "PORTLAND!" It could easily have been Oregon or Maine. We all chuckled as he waved us through and wondered if the officers even knew where Tennessee was. Ma Richards visited our farm several times with her daughters. They all loved country music and Johnny Cash. I always gave them a tour of Nashville and once took Ma and Verline into Tootsies Orchid Lounge. I ordered a beer, and Mom sat stone quiet. After a while perusing the clientele and patrons, Mama said, "I'm in the throes of hell."

When Ma Richards saw Doris and me on the stage of the Ryman one Saturday night, I could do nothing wrong. Back then, you needed to know the man working the door of the famous Ryman Auditorium of Nashville.

I have mentioned my brother, Harold. Not only he was a fellow Gemini, born May 11, 1931, his charm and good looks made him a hit with the public. Tragically killed at the age of 28, his star never got to shine. After his stint in the Navy and becoming a more accomplished musician, he was "antsy" to become known. He had just gotten a spot on the early morning wake up television WAVE in Louisville, KY and was honing his skills. He commanded a nightly spot-on Saturday night at the Mt Washington barn dance. I shall remember the morning around 2:00 o'clock AM, awakening the house with a drunken couple he had met in a Nashville gin mill. Mom, Dad, Bob and I were in bed fast asleep. The old upright piano in our living room had never heard the work out as the woman banged out "The birth of the blues," and she is singing in the still of the morning. They all three reeked of stale bourbon. I don't recall the details, but Mom was as nice as the occasion may be, but I don't think she offered them breakfast, and things were a bit icy for a length of time. I felt as a child a bit sorry for Harold as he didn't think he did anything wrong! I knew right then. I wanted to be just like Sherman Harold Payne when I grew up.

George Thomas or Tom. Tom and I were near strangers. He was nearly 19 years older than me. He was in service stationed in Germany when I was born. He went to Indianapolis for work, and we didn't really connect until the late seventies. I trained him in sales for Bel Air, was his power of Attorney, and in charge of his funeral. He treated me as a son rather than brother.

Ann and Dick had built their new home in Portland shortly before I was discharge in 1966. Being a boiler maker, Thomas commanded a good salary. The obstacle was that he had to do extensive travel and would be gone for long periods of time. Ann always had a very responsible and well-paying job. After Washington and the Pentagon, she worked at Gallatin Steam Plant, and later as an Accountant or,an Executive Secretary at Tennessee Gas Pipeline in Portland. She was the only female and worked for 20 or so males. They had her spoiled rotten. Ann had an exquisite taste. Not only in her dress, had done modeling in Nashville and later in Washington. She was selected to pose with a male model, taking dictation to appear in many small-town newspapers across the country. This was to encourage young girls newly graduated out of school to move to Washington and work for the Federal Government. My father carried around in his hip pocket for weeks a copy that was published in the Upper Sumner Press. Never ceasing the opportunity to pull it out and say proudly, "THIS IS MY DAUGHTER." This embarrassed my mother.

I was in and out of Western, had a shiny new sports car, wonder lust to get the hell out of Portland, and needed a job. Bel Air is thriving and growing nationally. Ann always liked having extra cash for something she normally wouldn't buy. The Franklin Church of Christ was having a pictorial directory. Fred suggested we give it a try to pass proofs. We used 35 MM slides and had to have a projector to show the proof. Both nervous, she and I alternated our spiel and sales technique. It must have worked because we both made $100 dollars in less than 4 hours. This was not 'bad change" in 1968. Ann was grateful to buy that expensive lamp she admired, and I was TOTALLY HOOKED.

We always had a menagerie of animals on the farm. We never bonded closely with them because they could become our food supply in the fall. We also had geese, ducks, and peacocks, as well as a large population of Rhode Island Reds and Plymouth Rocks. Cats were relegated to the barn to control the rat and mice population. When I was four or five, a beautiful adult Samoyed dog appeared at the farm. I was allowed to name him Shirley. Where I got that name, I shall never know as I was "what five" and didn't know it also could be a male name. We bonded quickly, and he was not only my baby sister but my best friend and protector. I taught him many tricks, and he lived to be a long age. We also had a white miniature poodle named Fifi that lived at least fifteen years. After Shirley died, we had rough collies. The most famous that comes to mind in a male named Pal, that was most famous playing a female on the famous television show Lassie. Our three were identical to Pal. They were ideal for the farm as they had full range. Our first was Colonel and then Ranger, and the last Thresher. Colonel was killed by a racing motorist, and Mom grieved until we replaced him with Ranger.

Bob was 5 years older than me. He had a subdued manner and was cunning. His dry wit was uncanny. We always had a sibling rivalry, but I was his best man at his wedding. Sadly, Bob was killed on an ice and snow-bound Jones hill about a ½ mile from home on Jones hill down from the family farm on Jan 6, 1995.

The following article called the BEST OF TIMES, was written by me for Billy and Janet Corkran for their 50th anniversary in California.

BEST OF TIMES

My earliest memory of Billy and Janet together happened at our farm in Tennessee. One afternoon, while they were visiting Mom and Dad, I was leaving for my junior prom date, probably in the spring of 1959 or 1960. I was one cool cat with a flat top haircut, a white linen jacket with a pink carnation, tuxedo pants, black tie, with black patent leather shoes. Can you image? I had white tube socks! (Probably cotton to boot) Janet, always the class act, rose to assure me that I would be the sharpest dressed person there. In Portland at the time, I probably was. I still have the photograph of shame to this day. BEST OF TIMES. (Note: Janet met Billy at Eastern Airlines and was a pioneer air hostess, as they were called.)

My fondest memories of Janet and Billy were picking me up at the Port of Authority or Grand Central Station in the fall of 1964 while I was temporarily based for deployment to Germany at FT Dix, NJ. It was my first trip to New York. In the Corvair with a carload of kids, I treasure the visits to East Norwich and Oyster Bay, going to mass with Janet at the local church, seeing the massive estates on Long Island, and I still can taste those delicious Manhattans that Billy made. Those were the BEST OF TIMES in my life.

For more years, we shared happy times with Grandma and Evans, our families, the good and bad, and AH, the wheat thrashings, including Janet's stepmom, Marie and Aunt Marg, from England, enjoying port wine at a pre threshing cookout on one visit. And do not forget the "hog killings" plus Steven, Chris and Tommy on the tractors. Also, I remember visiting you multiply times in Concord and the Bay Area, Rufus eating my sandwich off the plate, unbeknown to me, while I was hugging and saying hello to the kids and Amelia. Janet fixed me another with the same plate! We have been blessed in recent years to have you visit Nashville for the Raiders-Titans games and share more reunions. Again, THE BEST OF TIMES.

Billy, I still tell the story about running out of gas in front of Johnny and June Cash's house. Kate West picking us up in her bathrobe and house slipper after 200 AM at their pool house-lawnmower gasoline can in hand.

Whenever together, be it in Tennessee, New York, or California, Janet and Billy, you have always made me feel welcome. Our families share a special bond. There are never hours to get all the stories told. It is easy for me to say, "You are my favorite cousins." Not only for today, Oct 1, 2008 but for every day, I raise my glass to you. May God shine down on you richly with his blessings and joy. May you be granted many more years of the BEST OF TIMES in your life}

Margaret Pirkle Pirtle

Sarah Ann Elizabeth Perdue (daughter of Daniel Perdue)

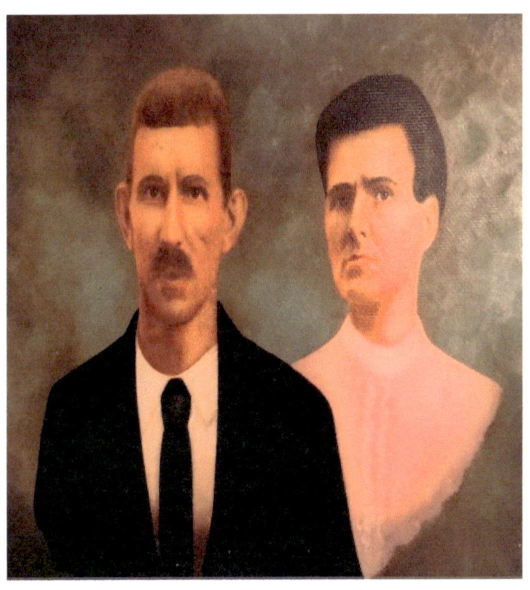

Lillie Mary Marlin and Albert Johns

James Elias Johns

Catherine Bunch and George W. Witham

Lily Mary Marlin Johns and children, 1958

Lillie Marlin Johns feeding a lamb

George Witham Payne, age 21

Fred, George W, Verline, Thomas C, Anna, Kathy, Jack, Bob and Harold, Easter Sunday, 1958

Verline, Anna, George T, Fred, Jim, Bob and Jack

Anna, George T, Fred, Jim, Bob and Jack, 4th of July

Anna, Pentagon, Washington, D.C. depicting taking steno for a national advertisement to encourage young ladies to consider work in Government after high school during World War II

Harold (Hal) Payne recording Honkey Tonk Stomp

James (Jim) Payne family

Brother Bob, Gloria, Laura, Lanna and Leigh Anne Payne

The next generation: Shepherd, Brody and Jovie Polk and Baylor Short

Jack with the oldest of the next generation and older brother to the triplets, Ezekiel (HossFly) Polk

Janet and Bill Corkran

Aunt Etta Brawner and Lillie Johns

Brother Fred and Mamie Payne

Brother George T Payne with sons Tracey and Stacey

Sister Anna with Thomas C Short

Sister-in-law Marjorie Payne

Family get together with brothers and cousins on the lake at Maui Manor

Chapter Nine: Payne family 4th of July Wheat Threshing

In the early 20th century, “combining and threshing” was the means that farmers had to get their grain crops processed and housed. I barely remember my family and neighbors going from farm to farm to do this. Much like hog-killing time, neighbors took care of neighbors. For two, the Gregory family had a steam engine, and we had a binder. When modern combines came onto the scene, they replaced the “age of steam,” and the old fashion method became passé. Uncle Evans Johns had a modern Allis Chamber combine, and I barely but vividly remember “tying sacks” every summer after I got old enough. Bob preceded me in the task, and I’m sure some of my Scott cousins worked for Evans. Oat chaff was always the worst when blended with sweat.

Fred and my older siblings treasured those memories. Fred had purchased several antique machines, including at least two Keck Gonnerman Steam engines combined. Bel Air was thriving well, and he enjoyed getting away from the stress and “unwinding” almost every weekend at the family farm in Portland. Sometimes, he would join forces with our cousin Dan Corkran, who had purchased the Corkran ancestral home in Portland. He, like Fred, liked to get away from a stressful and hectic job flying planes as a Captain for Eastern Airlines. It was also more than a treat for Verline and for her to be in her element, to cook, and to have a family home.

Fred sowed wheat in the winter, then combined and shook the grain when it was ripe in late June to thresh on the 4th of July. All of this is done for fun and relaxation. What began as a day to have a family reunion for neighbors to bond, quickly grew through the years to 400/500 people attending. I am not certain how many threshing’s were held; the records have been destroyed. The last one was in Tennessee’s Bicentennial year of 1976. At least two were held before my dad died on August 28, 1970. He was graveling with some fishing tongs in a newly dug well at Bob’s new house for a dropped tool. He passed quickly from a heart attack. The event was never the same without him. The first threshing was at the Freedle farm with Duke and Dick Freedle hosting. It was then moved to the Payne farm and expanded. "Gee, did it ever!"

The church's pictorial business is slow in the summer months. I would normally come home during the last week of June, on workdays and nights. The yard had to be cut and hedges manicured, plus Mom wanted all her flower beds up to speed. Our yard was a picture-perfect opportunity with strutting peacocks and our Tennessee walking horses behind white wooden fences. All this was being under the watchful eye of our collie dog, Colonel. I oversaw the meal and crowd control for the event. I would drive Fred's station wagon to Sam's warehouse in Nashville on the day of the 3rd. Mike Searcy, Kim, or Kathy sometimes were in tow. Gallons of lemonade would be mixed in 50-gallon trash barrels. Except for one year when we butchered our own hog at the Hudson farm, we had the bar-b-cue (the main course) catered. The first few years we prepared for two hundred people to eat but it added more each year. Most everyone that planned to eat would bring a side dish to add to the fare. We assembled three to four farm wagons under the large hickory and walnut trees in the side yard. One was for the band and singers and would be draped in red, white, and blue bunting. Two wagons were covered with white sheets for the food and a third wagon for the deserts. Kathy and Kim and later Pam were always eager to serve the drinks. That mantle was later passed on to Laura, Lanna and Angie. Fred, being a musician, was well connected in the music community in Kentucky. Herb Clinard and his K.Y. Brushfire Bluegrass Band were red hot. They came almost every year and said it was their favorite yearly venue. Wilkinson &Wiseman Funeral Home always provided 100-plus chairs to be placed near the band wagon. Parking was a nightmare, but with the horse lot open, it easily accommodated 50 cars or trucks. The threshing operation was a "well-coordinated effort." It could not have been done without the help of The Freedlemen, Bill Riggsbee, Vernon Griffin, and a host of others. One year, Thomas C., in the boiling sun, re-welded all the boiler units in one of the engines. What was designed for fun was a hot and sweaty, grueling job. Separating the grain from the husk to make a heaping straw stack was hard work. Many people would bring their pony carts for rides, and we could always depend on Carny Kilgore bringing his matched sorrel mules and wagon from Adams. Some would drive their antique cars or bring their tractors. The Nashville television stations always covered the event. We would gather in the living room after the masses had thinned to see the coverage on the 6 o'clock news, switching from channel to channel. One year, all three major stations cover the threshing. My favorite interview was the year that I interviewed Mom and her ringing the dinner bell to summon the field hands to eat. She handled the interview like a trooper. "Mrs. Payne, how do you feed 300 people?" "I host," she deadpanned! The Tennessean and local newspaper always chronicled the day. It was always a field day, especially election years for the politico.

It was clear the threshing had grown to a point it was too hard to pull off. Mom was getting to the point where it was difficult for her to have that many people in her space. She would gripe for days when people stepped on her flowers. Many people didn't respect her property, and we would pick up trash for days. The house was posted (closed), but strangers would still go inside. Invariably, the plumbing would be backed up for days. I don't know why we never had "port-a-potties" for the crowd. The cost of hosting the event had more than doubled, and it was twice the work. Enthusiasm had waned from all of us and practically from me. Plus, Daddy had died, and the threshing was not the same. It was hard work, folks!

It was a wonderful era of my life that I should treasure all the days of my life, but I regret that the "now" generation will never feel that fellowship and love we experienced on that one day in July every year.

The Payne wheat threshing is showcased in a three-page spread in REMEMBER WHEN PORTLAND AREA volume one (1) book published by the Portland Leader.

by Brenda Minor

Whether you spent Independence Day shooting fire crackers, eating watermelon or just sittin' on the porch in the cool shade—America's 202nd birthday is now history, and you are left with only the memory of exploding fireworks, juicy melons and hot dogs.

But the folks in Portland have a little more than the average Fourth of July celebration to commit to memory...The Annual Payne Farm Wheat Thrashing Picnic.

Mrs. George Payne and her family, five sons and a daughter, sponsor the yearly affair for the surrounding community of Portland.

This years' crowd totaled around 600 people and apparently everyone enjoyed the festivities and hospitality of the Paynes.

The youngest member of the family, Jack Payne, said the event was originally a family reunion. But when his father purchased a steam engine wheat thrasher "the neighbors came with a dish of food and helped with the chores of gathering the wheat. The event has blossomed into a more or less symbolic event and a community effort."

In keeping with the tradition the steam engine trashers were rolling and gathering the golden grain.

In addition to the farm machinery and mule drawn wagons were pony rides, hay rides, and a country music band and food galore.

The Herb Clinard Band "Brushfire," from Louisville, Kentucky provided foot stompin', knee slapping rhythm.

Candidates for the local election race took advantage of the opportunity to talk politics.

Some of the handshaking hopefuls included Dink Newman, James Dorris, T. Tommy Cutrer, William Woodard, Ruth Hassell, J.B. Rippy, Mahailiah Hughes, Jimmy England, Mayo Wix and representatives from the Clement campaign headquarters.

The country-type feast fed approximately 400 according to Jack Payne.

The meal consisted of barbecue, fried chicken, vegetables and home-made lemonade, and to begin the buffet style meal Mrs. George Payne summoned the crowd by ringing the dinner bell.

Politicians, musicians and farmers along with the Butchers, the Bakers and the picture-takers all set in the shade, talked -laughed and celebrated the birthday of our country as the tradition at the Payne Farm in Portland.

Bob Payne on the thrasher and George W Payne sacking grain

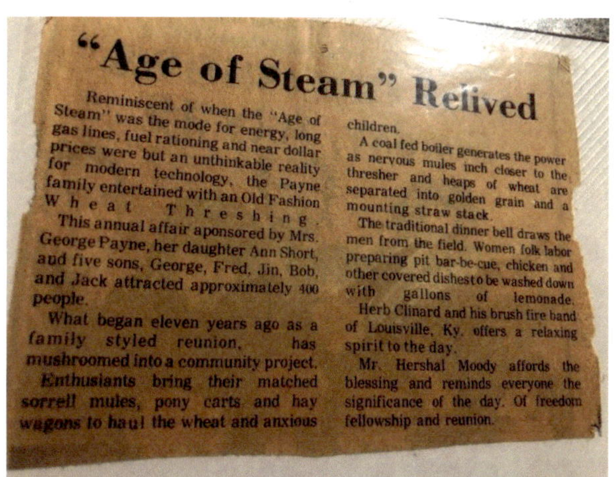

"Age of Steam" Relived

Reminiscent of when the "Age of Steam" was the mode for energy, long gas lines, fuel rationing and near dollar prices were but an unthinkable reality for modern technology, the Payne family entertained with an Old Fashion Wheat Threshing.

This annual affair aponsored by Mrs. George Payne, her daughter Ann Short, and five sons, George, Fred, Jin, Bob, and Jack attracted approximately 400 people.

What began eleven years ago as a family styled reunion, has mushroomed into a community project. Enthusiants bring their matched sorrell mules, pony carts and hay wagons to haul the wheat and anxious children.

A coal fed boiler generates the power as nervous mules inch closer to the thresher and heaps of wheat are separated into golden grain and a mounting straw stack.

The traditional dinner bell draws the men from the field. Women folk labor preparing pit bar-be-cue, chicken and other covered dishes to be washed down with gallons of lemonade.

Herb Clinard and his brush fire band of Louisville, Ky. offers a relaxing spirit to the day.

Mr. Hershal Moody affords the blessing and reminds everyone the significance of the day. Of freedom fellowship and reunion.

Age of Steam

Angie Hunt: America the beautiful, Payne Farm 4th of July wheat thrashing

Brother Fred and sister Anna cutting wheat in preparation for wheat thrashing

Chapter Ten: Bel Air Studios

At some point, all of us siblings worked for Bel Air Studios. Ann worked the least amount. She had Kathy and Tommy at home and Thomas C. much on the road. Thomas traveled extensively as a boiler maker welder, and she had a secure and responsible job in Portland. She was only "moonlit" for Bel Air if she or the kids wanted something special that was not in her regular budget. Ann had excellent taste, both in her dress and her home decor.

Fred had started Bel Air Studios with only two employees, and they are being part-time at that. I shall never forget George Deckman and Gene Rice. George was full-German from the West end of Louisville. George had a near-zero personality but was loyal as clockwork. He became a master at taking photographs. I learned later that, with my company, one can overlook flaws in people if they possess loyalty to you and your business. Gene was also a class act with too much rouge and a bit brassy! I loved her. She had a personality personified and was a major asset to his growing business. Fred's company was the first to pioneer church directories. He started locally in Louisville, one church at a time. Good work and word of mouth were the best advertisements, and he quickly mushroomed into a million-dollar industry. When I started working, as I had that night in Franklin with Ann, I was considered a proof consultant. The money was excellent, the hours short. It was adventurous to travel from city to city, state to state. I got to stay in the best hotels and eat in the best restaurants. I didn't have to be at work until most of the time, 4 PM. This allowed me to carouse at night, sleep late, and explore the city before work. Some of the consultants were bored housewives, and many, like Ann, wanted to supplement their family income. They also relished the short hours and excellent pay.

I worked in the airline industry for nearly 16 years. Even though I can tell good airline "war stories," some of my Bel Air travel days were ones for the books.

Nearly missing flight connections and navigating airports were sometimes a nightmare. At the acme for Bel Air's success, we were working coast to coast with satellite studios in many states. I was booking, training new photographers and proof consulting, doing photography, and the main "fire putter outer"! We even did the Shrine Temple directory in Honolulu. Bob lucked out on that assignment.

Once, I was rushing to make a flight, going God knows where from BNA. As usual, I am running late. As I neared the escalator to take the upper level to the gates, I noticed the stairs had been sealed off. The escalator was the only way. As I entered, contact papers were placed at every step. I'm taking two steps at a time, each time picking up the paper. As I neared the top, looking more like a dough boy and cursing like a sailor, I noticed a crowd of people down the hall staring. Approaching with a microphone was the MC for the T.V. show Candid Camera. He is following me to my gate. I am ripping off the contact paper and still cursing. I signed a release for it to be on television, but I never saw the clip. They would have had to heavily edit my language. I think that was probably around the same time I missed a Braniff flight to DFW or MIA. It was hijacked to Cuba. I vaguely recall that Tex Ridder and Ms. Charlie Nickens, the BBQ kingpin's wife, might have been aboard. When it happened, I lied and told everyone I was on the flight! I was never actually in Cuba, but I have flown over it and could feel like I could touch the palm trees flying to Jamaica. I expected Castro's regime to shoot us down at any point, seriously.

In another experience, Fred called me on the spur of the minute to tell me to go to the airport. A disgruntled minister in Albany, GA, was not happy about a makeup date. He thought he had been slighted by photography scheduling and demanded someone be at his church to do additional photography on Sunday morning. Fred couldn't reason with him, so he finally committed my services without checking with me first. That happened often. I'm scrambling, throwing cameras, lights, stands, and everything into a Samsonite suitcase to make the last Eastern flight to Atlanta to connect to Albany. As I approached the gate agent, I told them that I had delicate camera equipment and would gladly pay for it to be stored on the plane. They assured me that it was no problem; however, the plane was nearly two hours late. It was Saturday and Derby Day, and the plane was coming from Louisville, with a pit stop here and then on in Atlanta. There was no way I could make the last connection, but the minister must have had enough clout that he had the connection delayed for me. That would not happen in today's airline climate. Anyway, here comes the plane; the agents conversed with the flight attendant, and she assured me that my equipment would be in good hands even if she stowed it in a seat. Here comes the captain. He is totally pissed because he is two hours late and shows his ass. He demanded that I purchase another ticket and get a seat for the Samsonite. I have never seen a pilot openly argue with crew mention, and by now, the Eastern station agent in BNA is in the fray. It was so heated that the flight attendant kept bringing me drinks on the flight to Atlanta, even though I was being met by the minister in Albany. When we arrived in ATL, the station manager met me personally, apologized for the pilot's actions, and personally drove me by car to the commuter gate. I am sure that also played heavily that the Albany flight was delayed. I don't know if the pilot was reprimanded or not, but the BNA manager met my returning flight when I came back that next Monday morning.

Once, I had a last-minute presentation scheduled in Cleveland for an early morning. The only way I could make the meeting was to fly into Canton-Akron and rent a car. Getting in very late in Canton, I was starved to death, finally finding a last-minute hotel. As I checked in, I asked what restaurant would still be serving. I was directed about two blocks away. As I had had luggage stolen previously in Atlanta and St Louis, I dropped my bags off in the room and proceeded to the eatery. It is nearly empty and close to midnight. I noticed the restaurant crew was staring at me and talking to a fierce man who looked like Mafioso. It was obvious that I was the focus of their conversation. The waitress came over and asked if I was driving a white vehicle. She then adds, they are towing it off. I jumped up, ran out of the restaurant, and was nabbed by at least four policemen. There are blue lights everywhere after I exited. It seems there had been a child abduction that had just happened. The perpetrator was driving an identical vehicle with almost the same tag number. I'm trying to explain that I have just arrived. They were having none of my explanations. The only thing that saved me was that I pointed to the car rental sticker, and they called the hotel and verified I had just registered. I did make the meeting the next morning in Cleveland, but I have never been back to Canton/Akron.

I worked in a high-volume production market, either photographing or showing proofs to hundreds of families weekly while crisscrossing the country. Bel Air was now nationwide, and with the wonderful service he performed, cash had to be generated. It afforded me an education that I couldn't get at Western. I met different economic and social strata daily. Also, I learned a great deal about churches and their tenets. In one, I could be offered a beer in their fellowship hall after work, and then the next day, 300 miles always condemned me for wearing jewelry or expressing my church affiliation.

As I stated in the preface of my journal, it is not my desire to defame or hurt anyone in my account. I shall alter cities and names, but a couple of stories would make good "movie fodder." It was pretty much the rule of thumb that the more prominent the town citizen, the more eager to be in the directory. This always seemed to apply to doctors, lawyers, and car dealers. I always had a hostess to write the names of the subjects and introduce me to them. Most of the time, it was the designated committee chairman. Depending on the size of the shot and the days I would be working, I would become friends and make some life-lasting friendships for those unions. We always suggest they check a mirror before going in front of the camera. Once, out west and in a large prominent church, one of the town society matrons came in to be photographed. She had "beer can size" rollers in her hair. Several. The hostess gently suggested she go take them out. She replied, "Oh no, I have a banquet tonight, and I want my hair to look its best." I guess she didn't take into consideration that the photo would be viewed for generations and seen by thousands of people. In another large church in a different city, a well-dressed middle-aged man came in. He was carrying a large doll. He proceeded to preen the doll and even gave its name to the hostess. Little did I know, he had created the brand and became a multimillionaire marketing it in the 70ies. I wish I had a copy of that directory or, better yet, one of the "cabbage patch" dolls.

I was still relatively naïve then, even after military years and my worldly travels. I knew very little about the Trans-sexual community. It was a large, beautiful church, highly conservative with its strict doctrine, in an unnamed city. The committee chairman had told me that "Ethel" and "Fred" were pillows of the church, but different! I didn't have a clue what she meant as they were well dressed and looked "normal." Having just ten minutes to perform miracles is a science in some cases. Normally, I have the lady put her purse on a chair, sit on a piano bench on the left side, have the husband struggle on the bench, and sit on a couple of books to give him height. I asked for first name only, even if there were 15 people in the photo. It is uncanny how you can memorize names and have total recall two weeks later without missing a person's name. Bob and I always "went on one" with that ability. Back to the scene. "Ma'am put your purse there and please sit here." ME: "Ethel, please move your legs to the right as I am gesturing." SHE: "I'm not Ethel." I'm still in "La La Land," concerned about where the best bars in town are. When I get off, I ask the three-pieced-suited gentleman to straddle the bench. As I showed him how, he said, "I'm Ethel, and that is my wife, Fred." I just about lost it but calmed down enough and got some excellent portraits and got to show their proofs to them two weeks later. If I recall, they purchased our largest package available.

I found that the more conservative and strict values the rural churches shared, the better the stories I garnered. In most churches, we should be there on their fellowship night, and they always feed us well. Once in the very rural south, I met the most beautiful and genuine people that I shall never forget. Extension cords had to run from the adjoining parsonage to a room in the church that didn't have electrical service large enough to accommodate our set up. It was the hottest day of August. The committee chairman was the Pastor's wife. She had a gold star in her front tooth in her portly body that gleamed in the sun. She held up a dated, worn fur stole. "MISTUR PAYNES! I want all my church ladies to wear this FURRR piece in their portraits!" If I ever danced with charm, I did then; that was she sure she wanted her mink to be worn by so many in the intense heat, and some ladies might be offended that she was pushing her wrap on them when some couldn't offend it!

One of my hardest lessons was learned early in my career. Having studied art in college has led me to become a good photographer. We were still using Nikons and photographing with 35MM. I was dispatched to Phoenixville, Pennsylvania. It is one of the posher areas of Philadelphia's main line. I had photographed family members of Princess Grace Kelly, The Eisenhower family, and many other blue-blood families. After perhaps photographing 50 or more families, I discovered I had left the lens cap on the camera. I acted like nothing was wrong and continued to finish the assignment, but the damage had been done. The bulk of photos had been taken the previous day, Sunday. It was the hardest point of my life to return to Kentucky and face Fred. I begged not to return to rectify my mistake. In the end, it worked out that they photographed even more people and elites on the makeup date. I never left a lens cap on a camera again nor ever returned to the Main Line.

Just like my travels, I couldn't possibly mention every event, but I seemed to get a memory of every city and church I worked at.

Not all my experiences were negative. I was working a job in Monroe, LA, and had the weekend free. The airline was offering a $25.00 flight to Big Easy, New Orleans. I stayed at the Monteleone Hotel and got to see and meet Marlene Dietrich. It was her closing night at the Famous Blue Room at the Roosevelt Hotel. I have an autographed photo of her. At her close, the stage was bombarded with roses.

I was always eager to seek out the local attractions and meet the local people. It was educational to see how the cultures differ from state to state.

Working with Sarah Keeney was always an experience. We were partners in crime and were more like brothers and sisters than coworkers. My first recall of Sarah was at my brother Harold's funeral. She was older, a stout girl with a melodic singing voice to boot. She had on a long fur coat and oversized dark sunglasses, riding in a pink Cadillac. I thought that she was worldly. Little did I know, when she sang "More" for me, a G.I. in uniform from Ft. Harrison in Indianapolis, at the Louisville 1880 Club, we one day would work together. She went to Hawaii for a two-week vacation and stayed a year and a half. She headlined at the Anchor Club on notorious Hotel Street in Honolulu. We gathered many memories and always could create fun on the road. We did silly things that normal people would think strange. We would get a six-pack of beer, a pin, and a pad, and at Christmas time, we would drive through neighborhoods and critique house Christmas lights. We called ourselves the "Christmas light police." Seeing the names in mailboxes, "Mrs. Jones, please don't be offended; we feel that if you unlighted the small tree on the left side of your house, changed the red bulbs to white, etc., your display would be more outstanding. We sincerely wish you a Merry Christmas." Signed: The Christmas light Police. We were never caught, but tampering with mailboxes alone would have gotten us in a heap of trouble and totally disgraced Bel Air Studios. We would always decorate one of the rooms we were staying in for the award shows, complete with poo poo's and champagne. We attended the Kentucky Derby at least three times. Once in Millionaires Row, once in the Terrace, and the third time in the Infield. Millionaire's Row was better. Being a well-known entertainer, Sarah was well-connected and got favors. The year we sat in Millionaires Row, we sat next to the Turners, the owners of Dollar General Stores. Purely by coincidence, Mr. Turner and I had identical white suits, complete with dark blue shirts and almost the same identical bow ties. I regret that I didn't have a photo taken of us together. Our beautiful Schermerhorn Symphony

Home is named for Ms. Laura Turner. Ginger Rogers, Phyllis Diller, George Strait, and many more Hollywood likes were within eye sight from our box. Again, Millionaire Row is better. Sarah and I had many trips together. We went to Mexico, Hawaii, and Las Vegas, just to name a few. In every town we would hit, we would scout out if there was a piano bar. I was her pimp, and before long, she would be belting out the standards.

Roy Topps was a "huge" entertainer as well as in statute. Roy was 6 feet 7 in his stocking feet and nearly 300 pounds. He had played Tevye in "Fiddler on the Roof" and many other stage productions. He also appeared nightly at Suzie Wong's piano bar in mid-town Atlanta. This was the haunt of everyone from hookers to Atlanta "cream de la cream!" I was introduced to Roy by Doug Mann, who played the organ for the Braves Games. I met Doug years before he moved to Atlanta, and we continued our friendship after he relocated there. One outstanding memory of Susie Wong was shared one Halloween with Sarah. Roy had introduced me to Maynard Jackson and his lovely beauty queen wife, Valerie. He was then the current Mayor of Atlanta, and the Atlanta airport now bears his name, Atlanta Hartsfield/Jackson International. This was a far more tolerant race relations and politically correct era. Roy was giving two magnums of champagne to the best costume winners, and we had a week to prepare our getups. Maynard and I decided the week before (his idea) that he and his wife would come as Ku Klux Klansmen and Sarah and I as Mammie and Sammy. It was hilarious, and not one iota of feeling of racial or prejudice meaning. I had long hair, pleated it, and tied small bows, black leotards, a sweater, black gloves, a diaper, and a black face. Sarah wore one of her Hawaii muumuus, black face complete with a bandanna. I sat on her knee while she sang Mammie, and the Klansmen waved in the background! We got 1st prize and the four of us drank champagne on Roy the entire evening. Mayor Jackson was a good Mayor and advanced race relations for the city. This would be totally outrageous in this day and age, but there was a time when we all embraced each other with love. Little did I know that Roy, his family, and I would develop a beautiful and lasting friendship. Harriett was the matriarch of the family. She was a strong German woman in her mid-80s that could out work oxen. She possessed old-world ideas and ethics. She, with her three children, honed out an estate on two or three acres that was worthy of Architectural Digest. Roy, the oldest, designed Taliesin South, a cavernous two-level home with cantilevered balconies. They lived there from foundation to completion, struggling through some difficult, cold Atlanta winters. They broke bottles to fashion stain glass windows. They scoured every auction house and thrift store to find treasures for their mansion. Roy entertained the prisoners in exchange for art to amass a magnificent collection. It was patterned from Frank Lloyd Wright's Taliesin and could have a strong resemblance. I was fortunate to be invited for several weekends, and they were enthralled with Sarah and my antics and how we could out top each other with our yarns!

Mom never cared for Sarah and thought she was a bad influence. She would call her "Cargo" behind her back. Despite the name-calling, Mom always put on a pretense of liking her. She tolerated her because she worked for Fred and had been friends with Harold. I could write several chapters about Sarah. I miss her friendship every day.

Bob came aboard later. He was an excellent employee and could usually reason better than me, with sometimes a demanding schedule that came out of Louisville. The twins, Laura and Lanna, were small, but sometimes, Gloria would show proof of us. It was always fun when we worked together. We could always find a funny angle about most anything. Again, this was the 35 MM slide day. Once, I showed proof to a large, underprivileged family; they had a small child with health challenges. The child was not present, and I didn't realize she had facial and body deformities. I put one of her single-shot slides into the projector. There is this blood-curdling scream, SOSTOR, SOSTOR. I feel that I have put two slides in, and it is a double exposure. I took the slide out and inserted another. More screaming, "SOSTOR, SOSTOR!" Bob, in the next room, feared someone was hurt or in pain and came rushing in to see what had happened. One of the family members told me before he got to the door that this was the best picture Sister had ever made. When Bob appeared, he said, "Jack is everything OK?" I replied, "Yes, this is the best picture 'Soster ever made!'" We laughed about it later at dinner. He didn't forget it and even mentioned it later. Little did I know poor Lanna would be stuck with that moniker for the rest of her life? Again, no harm meant.

As I stated earlier, we had a knack for pet names for almost everybody. In early school, I was called "Sunshine." Years later, Brother Jim changed it to "Champ." Bob was called "Rose," Tom was "Roy," Jim was "Sue," Dad was "Cap," and Fred was "Teddy" and, years later, "J.R." for his entrepreneurial skills and a takeoff on Larry Hagman on Dallas. Tommy was "Larkin" or "Brewer." His grandfather, Larkin Short, died 111 years ago. Laura was called "Belle." She was named for her grandmother, Laura Veteto, but was called Belle for a neighbor named Laura Belle. Mom was nicknamed "Turk," Kim was called "Queen," and Leigh Anne was "Trip" because she was only 16 months older than the twins. Harold was called "Speedy" or "Speed." Thomas C, and for some reason, was called "Thomas Scissors?" Before my Uncle L. K. Johns was born, the midwife was certain that it was another girl. Counting my mother, there were four girls born to my Grandparents, Lillie and Albert Johns. Resolved it was another girl, Albert was totally floored when the mid wife said, Albert, "it's a boy"! The story goes Albert kept walking around and repeated, "I've got a boy, I've got a boy!" L.K. was called "Boy" until the day he passed. It is on his tombstone in Maple Hill. Uncle Bill, Mom's brother, was not very industrious. He was called "Moss Bill" because moss could grow on him as he moved so slowly. So, you can see, this habit of monikering names stretches generations.

I was getting weary of the extensive travel and monotony of the job and living in and out of motels and hotels. The travel to exotic places on the water made me determine if I ever had a home, it would be near water. It was also the inherited Witham genes as they were water people for generations. I realized I didn't have the financial strings of Bob, married, a mortgage, and small daughters. I felt I was being exploited with a never-ending schedule. One year was away for over 200 days with one stretch. I wanted to come home or at least spend more time at home. Fred also realized that Mom needed someone closer to help her. RiverGate Mall was new, and Fred seized the opportunity to open a (poster Shoppe) photography studio. He approached me about managing it. I couldn't resist coming home and having a chance to maybe buy a home. The decision was non-debatable.

Chapter Eleven: Bel Air Studios and Poster Shoppe Rivergate Mall

I was excited and found it fulfilling to be able to move back home to Portland and work at the Rivergate Mall in the fall of 1974. The mall was still new after a grand opening in the Fall of 1971. Fred had a summer poster shop in Gatlinburg, and Bob and I had alternated periods of time managing it. We had a leased chalet from the Ogles, and for the first time, it gave me a sense of independence. I felt a responsibility not to be in a different hotel room every week. There is something for sleeping in your own bed. The adage says you cannot ever go home. I found a since of security as I had never been away, coming back home to the farm, and living in Portland. Mom was needier with age, and it was a constant challenge not to have her monitor my comings and goings. Despite this, it was good that I could take care of the yard and help her with the groceries and upkeep of the house. At the same time, I was getting used to the routine of home life and wanting to invest in my own place to call my own.

The photography studio, despite the rent, was a booming success. We rented mall frontage space from McClellan's store. We started out basically as a poster shop doing 3 x 5 ft photo posters. This was a new art (photography) medium for Nashville, and we quickly aligned with the music industry and the entertainers. It was also a popular decorating choice for new restaurants. Mario the Italian ristorante in mid-town was a good account. Another was the Drag Queen performers on Hayes Street. We quickly expanded and relocated across to the other side of the store, expanding it to a Swiss chalet architecture style with hanging baskets of geraniums for a permanent full-service photography studio. I made many life-lasting friendships and got to photograph many celebrities and do lavish weddings, as well as many family portraits.

Bruce managed a men's store down the atrium among the many stores. He was always immaculately dressed and focused, and he didn't speak to anyone as he traversed the mall daily. The store manager's neighbors considered him eccentric and frugal and didn't want to seek his friendship. Well, the Gemini in me, plus fortifications with many Chico's margaritas almost daily, and my neighbor, partner in crime, Bill, knew there had to be a story line there. One day soon thereafter, Bruce was walking by the studio. Bill or I said hello. How are you today? That was all it took. We soon became close friends; he was simply shy, and he lamented for years that people were not friendly to him. Bruce was arch-conservative in his lifestyle. I never asked or hinted at how many resources he had or where he lived. I accepted the fact he was private with his lifestyle and felt he was comfortable with his means. He opened, closed, breathed the life of the store during mall hours, and didn't maintain a large staff but did the work himself. We soon became close acquaintances, and he would stop by the studio for coffee every day. After a year or so, he came by with a face that told me something was array. After questioning him, he blurted out.... "Jack: I, I, I just inherited (3) million dollars." WHOA! What does one say? His uncle, who was an inventor/investor in an international company based in Nashville, died. Bruce soon retired, bought the last made long black Cadillac, took a few world cruises, and moved into his uncle's beautiful home. I received an occasional postal card from him, but though he had moved on. One day, maybe less than a year, and totally out of the blue, Bruce appeared at my office. "Jack, I'm miserable. I am too young to retire and need a purpose. I need a job." He asked if I had a connection at the Mexican restaurant and if I could possibly put in a word for him. Felix hired him immediately. What was to have been three days a week, with a maximum of 24 hours per week, quickly changed. He worked almost daily and for many shifts for waiters needing or wanting time off. Bruce was truly a workaholic. We became good friends, and perhaps in a sequel to this account, I can add some of the escapades we shared.

Thelma Lou was a demure, blonde, gracious older lady who took care of the plants for Rivergate Mall. She and her sons had owned a landscaping and plant nursery in Nashville. I patronized their store for years, and I went to college with one of her sons. Bel Air Studio set had many life plants, and the front office faced the mall. This was a draw for Thelma. It wasn't long before we established contact and became fast friends. She kept all our plants alive and thriving far better than I could. She became part of our Maui Manner/Rivergate Mall posse, and we remained friends until her death. I miss her still.

I met many new friends while at Rivergate. Like with Bruce, we normally only spoke or waved to each other without much conversation. Rivergate had sidewalk sales a couple of times a year. The merchants were encouraged to set up their wares in the center of the concourses. Fred had recently closed the Gatlinburg shop for the season, and I had an ample supply of period costumes at the studio. Magnavox Music Center was directly across the concourse. For the fall sale, they had their best Hammond organ and best salesman, Mickey, in the fray. This was hand shaking distance from my camera in the middle of the mall. The headliner at The Embers in Printers Alley was Heaven Lee. She was shopping at the mall, and Mickey was cranking out Deep Purple on Hammond to draw a crowd. I dressed Heaven as a vintage saloon girl, with a black beaded dress lit to the waist red garter with feather boas. We almost had to call it crowd control. Anyway, Mickey is less than 5 feet from me. The crowd has dispersed. Long story short, he says, I wish I had a screwdriver. I was nursing one (screwdriver) as we spoke, and he couldn't believe I was drinking in the mall. Maybe he did believe it because we became life lone friends. I soon met his beautiful family and quickly established that his beautiful wife Sandy and I had history from past happy hours at one of my favorite downtown haunts. Bobby Jo Walls sang at the piano bar at the world-class Brass Rail Stables in Printers Alley. The building was originally stables for President Jackson when he came to town to law practice. Everybody from Sinatra, Dinah, Alice, Phil Harris, and even Spiro Agnew took their turn at her piano or microphone when in town. She could tell the neatest stories and how she cussed out a drunken "famous person" for almost chipping one of her teeth! We lost Bobby Jo far too soon to a tragic car accident while she was appearing in Atlanta.

This is out of context with my sequence of chapters, but Ted became part of our group during this era. Ted was country as corn, didn't have a strong command of the king's English, had little education, and was from rural McMinnville, but was a wiz and champion of plumbing and electrical wiring needs. This was the basis for friendship for me. He professed he had never been out of the state of Tennessee. I introduced him to Sara and Harry, and they equally loved and quickly adopted him with heart and soul and his content of character. They (We) plied him with stories of their (our) world travels, and his dark eyes would flash. One night, over a lot of liquor, we concocted a trip to Hawaii with his bucolic bearings. Ted had money. Once agreed, I picked Ted up to go shopping. Off we go to Cain Sloan Rivergate Men's Dept. The salesperson barely acknowledged us. Things quickly changed when I started our business and after spending $500.00 or more on his wardrobe. She is now Ted's best friend and was really kissing Ted's ass. In Hawaii, Ted saw sights he talked about for the rest of his life. The country boy came out of him when he was on the return flight home; he was sitting in front of Harry. He started butchering/cutting slits in his Florsheim shoes to give his bunions and corns some ease.

There was a very popular grille at McLellan's. It was the morning gathering place for morning joggers as well as for ardent shoppers. Jim G., or as Verline quickly deemed him (Rollers), the assistant manager, and I were on very good terms. He had broken a leg and was confined to a wheelchair for several months. He knew about my brass bed from "The House on Clay Street" in Bowling Green, Kentucky. Uncle Boy had helped me purchase it from one of Pauline's "whore house" estate sales. She retired, and her property had been closed, demolished, and sold for development. Niemen Marcus, the Tony department store in Dallas, knew the legacy of Pauline's house of ill repute and the success of the recently published book and purchased all the bricks from the demolition site. They polished each one, put a piece of felt on one side, and embossed on the other, "For a piece of history." Then, displayed in their Christmas catalog, bricks were sold for $100.00 each. I have the brass bed from her East room featured in the book, plus two copies of her book in my guest room. Jim knew my infinity for her and told me she took shopping pilgrimages to the mall. I was star-struck the morning Jim came over to my office. It was awfully hard not to stare. She had silky white hair piled in a bouffant tall beehive. I thought of Marie Antoinette. She had on a simple print and probably flowered gingham house dress. Something my mother would wear daily to do housework. Add to this the black old-fashioned maid oxfords that I remember Grandma wearing. The kicker, her skin looked like porcelain, and she had to be in her eighties. Her mouth was cherry cherub red with long fingernails painted as her mouth. She had large diamond rings on every finger. I regret until this today, knowing the "chutzpah" that I had and not going over and meet her. I could have taken her portrait. I was transfixed. When I say chutzpah, I had no reservations about having celebrates sit in a portrait or for a poster. I recall Rivergate, Johnny and June, Heaven Lee the stripper, Ronnie McDowell, Red Skelton, Grandpa Jones, Barbara Mandrell, Conway Twitty, Cicely Tyson, Bill Monroe, and Roy Acuff, just to name a few. I am still confident that my Uncle Boy's insistence on taking no for me to get the bed for a piece of history probably meant he got a "piece of history" on Clay Street! I still have the velvet red book displays and the brass bed from her east room.

Our favorite haunt at the mall was having margaritas at El Chico restaurant. I shall never forget Bill Hosey and his wild bunch of siblings. I had good employees, but I must cite Tom Rainey, whom I trusted and who helped him broaden his photograph skills. I never worried about leaving the place on Tom's watch.

Rivergate, like most malls, discouraged small businesses and preferred chain stores. The reason is every mall in the USA has a JCPenney or Sears or both, plus upscale department stores like Macy's. I say Macy's because it bought out most of the leading stores in larger cities. Rivergate was still new, and the Green Hills/

Brentwood/Franklin markets were a threat to their ability to stay with the national trends. That trickled down to the smaller stores, and we were small potatoes. The rent was astronomically high, and even though we were profitable at a large volume, we couldn't compete with the chain stores. McClellan's charged a king's ransom in rent, and we had to ultimately, for economic reasons, close. It was a wonderful run while we were there, and I cherish the time and friendships I made. I knew I would never go back on the road, and I had to have a means of support to keep me in Nashville. I still dreamed about working for an airline.

Chapter Twelve: Maui Manner / Friends and Neighbors

156 Sunset Drive, Hendersonville, TN. 37075: Purchased June 27, 1977 from Betsy Reed. After seeing the Mediterranean and Caribbean seas and the shores of Maui on the Pacific, I vowed if I ever had a home, it would be on or near water. This might have stemmed from my Witham genes, as they were generational "water people."

Wayne Beshears worked directly across from my studio at Magnavox Music Center. He was mild-mannered and a devout Christian. He, like almost everyone else, moon lighted in real estate sales. He knew my passion for getting a home. Wayne was under a false illusion that I had or came from money. I did have a few thousand bucks saved, but it would be considered peanuts now. I had made it clear that I wanted to go directly to the water on Old Hickory Lake, maybe a bit of acreage, and totally wanted a "fix me upper"! Wayne was on the scent and constantly would bring me showings that were totally out of my league. One morning, he called me early at the farm to summon me to meet him at the mall. Wayne, you better not be leading me on a wild goose chase. I chided. Sure enough, the property was Conway Twiddy's old Spanish-tiled mansion on Walton Ferry. He had just moved to his new complex, Twiddy City. I don't remember the listing amount, but it was more than a million. I cursed Wayne all the way back to the mall and the fact he had gotten me up so early. After the mall had opened and I was having coffee at my desk, Wayne came over sheepishly and plopped the Nashville multi-real estate listing book on my desk. Even then, it was over 6 inches thick. The book fell open in front of me. What do I see? An overhead shot of Maui Manner shows a flat white marble ship roof and a boat dock, which are listed as an acre. If I recall, it was $50,000. Wayne, I want to see this! No, it's in a bad area, and you don't want to see it. After arguing with him, and he was still reeling from my wrath, I threatened to call the listing agent myself, and he agreed to call the agent. A time was set to take a tour. It was very early in the morning in early June. The lake was totally shrouded in fog, and it reminded me greatly of

London. It was probably as well that I couldn't see some of the small and many unkempt houses on River Road. Even then, some of the cottages were used as summer fishing cottages. Arriving at the driveway at the top of the hill at 156, the entrance was totally barricaded. It was clear that strangers were not welcome. The fog was pea soup thick. As I stepped out of the car and just hundreds of yards across the lake, three tug boats and barges were snarled at the locks of the dam. They each sounded their horns in three different octaves, and I was in San Francisco or Bremerhaven again! I keep screaming, I've got to have this place! Wayne thought I had totally lost my mind. I have lived here for over 40 years and have not heard that total melodic medley since. It was a signal from God. As we made our way down the gravel drive way, I could barely make out that it was indeed on the water. To say it was in bad shape was an understatement. California privet had grown above the lakeside windows; water was standing 8 inches in the basement. It was designed for boat storage with a garage door. It had remnants that it had been used as a bed room and also had a plumbing for a toilet. The septic tank had been built on the upper side and had been punctured as it was in the drive way turn round. Raw sewerage seeped to the lower lever and on the neighbor's property. The flat roof, which was marble chips, though attractive, leaked. The electric was dangerous, and the tenants had to resort to electric skillets and space heaters. Wayne was appalled.

Driving back to River gate and near silence, I told Wayne to make an offer. I recall maybe $25,000. Wayne balked and said that was an insult and he wouldn't do it. Again, I played hard ball and told him I would call myself. To both of our surprise, the agent called within an hour with a counter offer of around $35,000. I can't recall the exact amount.

My neighbor in the mall was Bill Hosey. He had a jewelry concession next to our studio as a side line to his family business. We became good friends and as well also with his large family. Mr. Harry, Bill's Dad, was a business entrepreneur and was considered for an Embassy assignment in Haiti before the Kennedy assassination. They owned Old Hickory Manufacturing as well as Poplar Cedars Estate in Old Hickory, plus other vast holdings. I had the pleasure of photographing the Hosey family several times, and one great memory was of Bill's sister Maureen's wedding. It was pouring rain, but it was an upscale Catholic wedding on the grounds of Poplar Cedars. Bill was one of 14 children. Several of Bill's mischievous brothers released a goat just as the couple was slicing their wedding cake. It was as slight to see with the mounting mud women in designer gowns barefoot and trying to right the table and salvage the cake from ruin from the goat bolting under the table. I managed to capture it all on film. Bill's advice to me was to buy the property, even at the asking price, if necessary. It was the best advice anyone ever gave me.

Now to face Verline! Mother would have been pleased if I had never left home. She was secure that I was living at home, and I tried to respect her feelings. She hated my lake property and often referred to the Rockland area as West Virginia. I solicited Ann to be my go-between. I wasn't as lucky with the dense fog to camouflage the area the day I bought them to see the property. I didn't know the total facts about the seller at the time, but it was a sad situation. I shall not print names. What had been a summer get away lake cottage for a prominent Nashville surgeon and his family, things went south. It seems his wife had been embroiled in a salacious scandal. The Doctor divorced her, leaving little means of support. To combat this, she had terminal sickness in her family and was resorted to the late cottage with little or no income. Well, again, the entranced was blocked, but we managed to get Mom to the house. As she opened the door, a cat jumped over a hot skillet of cooking bacon in the bar area, burning a paw and screeching like a wounded bungee. The odor was over powering with cat and dog feces and urine. It took months for me to get rid of the odors. You could barely see the water from the 2nd story windows on the sun porch. The seller's friend looked like Ollie of Kukla, Fran, and Ollie puppets. She was tall, had large dark eyes and had one front tooth, unkempt in men's clothing, and had a deep husky voice. Ann and I surveyed the property with the owner, and Ann tried to be supportive and encouraging and offering positive tips that could be done. Mom was having none of the tour and found the cleanest chair to sit in. It was a very dry period of time with little rain. Left alone with the paramour, Mom tried to make some small talk. She asked if they had ever raised tobacco, etc. and if they had ever been on a farm. Driving home, there was silence. Somewhere around the ridge, Mom said, "That was the ugliest man I have ever seen!" Ann and I looked at each other, and finally one of us said that it was not a man! Mom was speechless the rest of the way home and sealed the deal that Mom never ever liked Maui Manner.

Relying on Bill's advice, I knew I had little to lose, and he said it was worth the original asking price. Wayne did counteroffer with $27,500, and to my delight, it was accepted, and I closed on my house on July 27, 1977. I often wondered what happened to the seller, but I didn't follow through with keeping up with her.

Much needed to be done before it was inhabitable. I had to have a new roof, which my Uncle Fred, a contractor, installed. He cautioned me that a flat roof of that type was a placebo. He gave me a good contract price but had fishing privileges for the rest of his life. The next step was a central heating and air conditioning system and rewiring. For several years, I lived on the top level but later installed a glass sliding door where the garage was, enclosed the downstairs open patio, and added a spiral staircase and French drain inside and out of the foundation. I doubled my living space.

In 1977, I was 34 years old. At that point, it was apparent that I would not ever get married. I was still living with my mother, but I also wanted to establish some boundaries of what I wanted for the rest of my life. Certainly, Portland was not in the plan. From an early age, Mom taught all of her sons to cook. "You never know when you are going to need it," she would say. Thank God she had that foresight, as it was needed for all of her boys later in life. Fred could probably "outdo" her on her cornbread dressing during the holidays. The original recipe had been passed down from my grandmother, Lillie Johns. Each of her daughters made variations. There is a talent for good dressing, and I have tried to tweak it but never, ever vary from the main ingredients. I have taught Kelly and Jordan the tradition and hope they will teach their children. Verline had that foresight, and thankfully, I cook and enjoy it. It brings me out of a funk when nothing else works.

Jack is weaning Verline, as Sarah Keeny would say! She knew that (Turk) didn't like her and tried to give gabs when she could. My new house was 5 minutes from the mall and at the farm more than 30 minutes in good traffic. The main reason, as I have stated, is that many repairs need to be done to the house. I guess Sarah, however, had a point because she would pout if I told her I wasn't coming home for the night from RiverGate. As time went one with the renovation and it became more livable, I began to spend more time at the house. I guess I got some sort of acceptance from my mother when Ann told her they needed to come and help scrub my Ponderosa pine for sealing. Perhaps she just wanted an outing? I still have the paneling in my dining room.

In the beginning, I made many lifetime friendships and good neighbor relationships. The die had been cast for me to be a gentleman from growing up on a farm in a rural area. I was friendly, helpful, and outgoing but always respectful of their spaces and properties. I was young, had extra money to spend, was healthy, and was interested in making my home beautiful inside and out. I strove to be a good neighbor and always wanted to improve my property as well as enhance the neighborhood. Bringing them fresh Portland strawberries every May also strengthens our friendships. I usually bought a crate and would knock on doors even with neighbors. I wasn't that bonded with them. In 1977, I was the youngest person on the point stretching from Rockland Road on River to Rice on the left to Sunset to the lake. I am now the oldest original resident, and every property has changed hands at least once, which I can identify. My next-door neighbors were Elrita and Rich Hewitt. They had lived in Madison, and he was retired from the Post Office. They bought and built their dream home on a stretch of land purchased from the Rush subdivision in Hendersonville. This was the first planed subdivision for the city of

Hendersonville. Ms. Hewitt didn't want to relocate from Madison. She felt that Hendersonville was primitive and beneath her social status. To appease her for the transition, he ordered a specific white brick for the design, and it had an Old New Orleans look, complete with lots of black wrought iron on the upper-level porch that spanned the entire length of the house. This was an imposing house for the new and budding Old Hickory Lake scene, and it was closest to the water with a commanding view of the dam. A wing that was referred to as the "mother-in-law" was added to the design to accommodate one of their elderly parents. This addition was less than 25 feet from my house. When I moved in, Miss Catherine Wiggers, an elderly Russian spinster, was in the residence of the mother-in-law apartment. She claimed direct heritage to Catherine the Great and the Romanoff family. She was a retired seamstress and had worked for Fred Harvey, Nashville's largest department store, for years. She was reclusive, a talented artist, and confined to the apartment. The shrubbery was taller than our houses, and she would sit in the lakeside window for hours. I immediately cut the hedges back to make some form of a hedge. This opened an entirely new window to the world for her, and she would sit peering out the binds. Occasionally, after dark, she would sidle out the door and stand for a long period. I befriended her, and we became good friends, and she would regale me with lots of stories. I'm sure most of them were true. A former war pal and best friend of Mr. Hewitt persuaded him to sell him a sliver of land to build a small retirement cottage. He agreed, and the same brick of the main house was used in the construction of the cottage. The only access was the rear driveway on the backside of the house. The friendship quickly fell out of favor; Rich was difficult, and the owner was now land locked to get off his property. Mr. Hewitt barred him from using his driveway. The new owner, to distinguish such a sort of border, had erected a chain-length fence to separate the properties. Elrita was not about to tolerate a chain fence and had California privet planted the length of the property lines. If contained, the privet makes an attractive hedge, but unkempt becomes a night mare. Now landlocked, the only way off the property was by the lake or cross several properties to the street. Feeling badly about his dilemma, Jim Freeman, with his new wife Nellie and adjoining neighbor on the right, sold him the width of the property to Sunset Drive from the property line and made it a rectangle for a full acre. The property line is within 5 to 6 feet of the Freeman house. To Mr. Freeman's dismay, the drive way was cut closer to his house. I soon introduced myself to the Hewitts when I purchased my place. She felt herself Patrician and liked to project her heritage of being a DAR docent, etc. She eyed me up and down and with a condescending nasal chide.... "Jackson, I'm Elrita Taylor Hewitt, 7th generation descendant of President Zachery Taylor of Kentucky, Daughter of et cetera, et cetera, and JUST who are you?" Without batting an eye, I replied that my Great, great, great grandfather was an officer for the Union while his twin brother served for the Confederacy, that my other Grandparents were equally Mayflower fodder, and was I ever on stage, spurring bullshit much as I had that Thanksgiving Day in Central Park West. I guess growing up poor in a rural town but having exposure to cultural lifestyles gave me a chance to project who I really was not. I had the male lead on our senior play, Mr. Beane from Lima, in high school. I received rave comments because I played the aristocratic Beane to the hilt. This explains better some of the 15 percent bullshit I referred to in the preface of my book. Little did I know then that I would spend years later researching my family genealogy. Being bound to my computer for long periods of time after several surgeries, I spent hours upon hours researching my heritage. Daddy had been robbed of his birthright, and I wanted to know the answers that had been hidden from him. Almost daily, the sun would be rising, and I would still be pouring through books and web sites. I totally contribute my sanity to this cause to help get me through the night. I now have extensive knowledge and proof of at least ten (10) families on both sides of my parents, most dating to Europe and Africa. With that performance with Elrita, Rich looked on sheepishly and grinned, and I felt I gained silent respect for him for standing up to his pompous wife. She, too, warmed to me, and we became good neighbors and later friends.

Doc West and his much younger wife Kathleen lived across the street. He came from old money and prestige. This was his retirement lake house, lavishly furnished with memorabilia from his career. He had served in the state Senate and owned a pharmacy, which is why he was called Doc. He considered himself a curmudgeon and had a strong appetite for liquor. He also detested Rich Hewitt. Doc called Rich horrible names and likewise. His prize and joy were Kathleen and his peach trees to make brandy in the summertime. He would shoot the squirrels, and Rich would call the police. Kathleen tolerated me, but I felt resentment toward my friendship with Doc. On December 24, 1978, I was readying myself to go to Sister Anna's house for Christmas Eve dinner with family. Elrita had called to tell me that Doc was in Madison hospital and in grave condition. Out of love and respect for him, I decided to stop to say goodbye. I found Kathleen in a dark room and Doc laboring from his breath. I had planned to stop briefly but stayed longer because of the sad situation. It was Christmas Eve, and he obviously was dying. Even though I felt she didn't care for me, I sensed her appreciation and that she cared. I told her I was available and should she need anything to call. During Christmas Day evening, I was playing scrabble with Mayme at Moms. Elrita called to say Doc had passed and that Kathleen had instructed her to call me first. She wanted to know if I was going to the visitation/funeral, and if so, she and Rich could ride. I had to come home and dress and pick them up. Elrita, totally swathed in black and with a beaver hat as large as an umbrella, looked like Norma Desmond from Sunset Boulevard. This was just for visitation. Several weeks went by, and we had several bouts of cold temperatures and snow. One Saturday afternoon, my phone rang. "Jack, this is Kate West. Could you bring some fire wood inside for me?" I immediately said yes and, upon arriving, found she had a bottle of wine opened. She apologized for misjudging me while Doc was alive and thanked me profusely for coming to visit during her lowest hour. Because lasting friends for her lifetime, I could tell many stories that we shared, but I will hit on two. I have said before that Billy was my favorite cousin. That can't be accurate, as I also told both Peggy and Shirley separately that they were my favorite. Again, more bull shit! Billy was in town from California, and while visiting me, Kate stopped by. She fell totally in love with him and likewise. She regaled him with stories of times past of the old Nashville and mentioned many famous people that Billy remembered from his youth. I had a brand new silver Pontiac station wagon, and Keepsake Portraits was doing well. I was king of the mountain. Later that evening, with a six-pack of beer, after touring my studio and downtown Nashville, we were back in Hendersonville. He wanted to see Johnny Cash, Roy Orbison, and other star's homes. I was totally in my element, and it never occurred to look at the gas gauge. Directly in front of the Cash house, I ran out of gas. It is nearly 3 AM. The car was in the center of the road. I was embarrassed that I could be so careless and trying to be so cool and suave with my older cousin. This was long before cell phones. I met Armando, the security officer in the guardhouse, at a function at the Cashes. He worked for Johnny for several years and was very devoted. I pleaded my case, and between the looks of the new car, Billy's coolness, and my dropping a few names, he agreed to allow me to use the telephone. The problem was the guard shack telephone was out of order. He relegated us to the pool house. It was an imposing structure built down front from the mansion and adjoining an Olympic-sized pool. It commanded a beautiful view of the lake. One of the singing Bee Gees, Morris Gibb, purchased the estate after the Cashes died and, during a renovation, it burned to the ground. With Billy and the guard in tow, we entered the unlocked pool house. "My God, Billy, who can we call at 3 AM?" Fortified with the beer confidence, remembering the new "kinship" they shared, we both said at the said time, "Kate!" The phone rang only twice. "Hello Kate, do you love me?" "Jack, are you drunk? Where are you?" "Yes, and we are in June Carter Cashes pool house. Does she ever have bad taste?" I thought Kate was going to hang up, but she got up, put a robe over her pajamas, got a can of lawnmower gas, and drove to our rescue. We later laughed about it, and it gave reason for Billy to ask about Kate every time he called me.

My favorite story with Kate was shortly after we became good friends. I was traveling for long periods of time and could sometimes be home for a week's stretch. Of course, I had to divide that time with Verline to make sure the grass was cut and her needs were met. The neighborhood seemed to know when I was coming home. I would turn every light on and stay up until the wee hours. I wanted some shelves that would hold my stereo components and books. I had an old red truck that was perfect for the junk heap. It was more rusted than paint and had holes in the floorboard, so you could easily see the pavement. How it made it back and forth to Portland amazes me still. How it yearly passed emission was even more of a wonder. A wheel actually came off in the middle of Gallatin Road, at rush hour traffic once whirling down the center of the road for a block at Center Point. No one was hurt, no cars were hit, and the truck was able to be driven when I got the spare back on. Talk about divine intervention. The muffler was louder than any race car at "The Brickyard." The passenger door had to be wired for anyone wanting to ride. I had a pretty good idea of what I wanted and felt I could get three (3 bookcases- for perhaps a hundred dollars each, and my budget was three hundred dollars. I had scouted three furniture stores, and one was in downtown Nashville. As I was pulling out of my driveway, Kate had just pulled into her front entrance. She hailed me down. I had been out of town for weeks, but I was on a pilgrimage to get my furniture. She had been to a tea or a social function and was dressed to the nines, complete in a full-length mink coat. I had long hair, cut-off shorts to my ass, and an old college WKU holey t-shirt. I told her of my quest, and to my surprise, she offered to ride with me. I wired her into the passenger side. Her coat was worth several times more than what my red truck would fetch. Sputtering down Gallatin Road, I had chartered the stores I wanted to stop. We would pass the upscale Ethan Allen House in Madison. Remembering my sister's taste, it was not in my sights. Kate was adamant that we stop and compare. I pulled up in the front of the store, rolling closer to the full plate glass windows because the brakes were not working well. Several associates were looking out, fearing we were going to crash through the store. I am sure they also had heard the truck from a city block away. I unwire Kate, and we proceed inside. You could see the clerks muttering with each other and pointing out to my truck. A man salesman who looked more like a mortician came up to inquire what we wanted to see. He showed us around, and the nearest thing that would have worked for me was a solid cherry $2000.00 plus cabinet. The man would look at me, my shorts, Kate's coat, and then out at the truck. Finally, I said. "Sir, you have been helpful and kind. We just got married yesterday and are starting out housekeeping. I don't make much money after just getting out of the pen. All she wanted for the wedding was that damn fur coat which I will never get paid off. I think we may be in the wrong store. I just don't believe our marriage was a good fit or will work out!" I had to get Kate rewired back into the truck before she peed in her pants, and the associates were in the front window, gaping as we drove away. We laughed all the way to John F. Lawhons on Jefferson Street. I got the cases for less than I had budgeted and still use them at Maui Manner.

I could not possibly attempt any writing without mentioning The Bell Cove Club. It is immediately across Sunset Drive from my property. It commands the most beautiful view and centers the main channel of the lake for perfect sunsets. The imposing log house structure was originally smaller. It was built as a lake retreat by an enterprising French lady. She had the first diaper laundering service in Nashville, invented Pampers, and amassed a fortune before retiring to Florida. It has served as a private country club, several restaurants, a nightclub, and a recording studio. It has served many owners over the years. "Woody" Woodward owned it when I came on the scene. His daughter Brenda and I became good friends. She had fiery red hair and spunk as well. Many times, when I would be home, she and her husband Buddy would close the club at 2 PM. They'd package up the leftover steak and bring it, usually with a band of leftover patrons, to my house. I have a vivid memory of poor Buddy, well over six feet, trying to sleep on my 5 five plus rattan settee. As Verline said about the boys bringing home "strays" for the night, I never knew how many bodies were at my house in the morning. Once, Kay Savage from Memphis, Jim Jenkins, and I went for three days to the new Opryland Hotel for a photography convention. It was a deep snow that stayed for a week. I had entrusted Brenda, Mickey, and a couple of others to keep watch on the house. Jim and I had to pick Kaye up at the airport, the last flight to land before closing, and we had a full party in swing before when we left. I called home late the next day, and the party was still in full swing. They truly were snowed in.

Dag Tasbagh and his family, a Shah supporter, migrated from Iran. It was embarrassing that the public didn't support the club during his tenure of ownership. The restaurant would get pelted with eggs, and people, in general, were unkind to him and his family and would boycott the place. I was not close friends with many of the owners through the years, but that changed in 1986 when Joy Ford purchased the Bell Cove Club.

Joy Ford should have a sole chapter. Without Joy and her Bell Cove Club, my book would be dull. Through Joy and her club, I have made life-lasting friendships. Joy was born in rural Alabama to a large family. I had the great pleasure of knowing her sweet mother, Velma, and her brother Allen. Joy and I quickly bonded, and we still attribute it to our Cherokee ancestry. She and I may go weeks, even months, and not see each other, a chance to meet and pick up where we left off. With her dark eyes, dark hair, and melodic voice talent, she ended up in New York City, where she met her prince charming Sherman. He was from New England and was very successful in publishing and music. When around Sherman, you could sense his devotion to her. They were in New York, but Joy's passion lay in country music. Where better to be based than Nashville? When it became available, they quickly seized the opportunity to purchase the Cove, and the rest is history. Sherman divided his time between his Arabian horse ranch in Charlotte, TN, the Bell Cove, and his International Music building on Music Row. Joy has always been very benevolent with her resources. She has helped many musicians establish careers that have earned world acclaim. Many famous people have made films, recorded, or performed on stage. For years, it was home to Bill Monroe. The same is true with her charitable contributions and access to the Bell Cove for groups to hold meetings. In August 1987, the Ray Cash Memorial American Legion Post # 245 was chartered. I was honored to be elected as an officer and later would serve as Post Commander. The dedication reception was held on the Terrace, and she allowed us monthly to meet while we sought a permanent home. I treasure the chance to have known Sherman and count Joy Ford as one of my dearest friends.

I am still the new kid on the block on Sunset Drive in the early 80s. I owned Keepsake Studios and had cash to burn. I met Anne West through her uncle, and my neighbor, DocWest. She and I became fast friends. Anne had a 1963 red convertible, and when it was cold, she always kept two mink coats in her truck. She said, one for sport and one for dress. "One never knows when the occasion may arise", to quote Anne. She now lives in Hendersonville, and we talk almost daily.

I was known for hosting good parties at Maui Manner in winter as well as summer. I would decorate for the day and serve period food. St Patrick's Day was always one of my favorites. Maybe it was the signal that warm weather was on its way. I had dyed green beer, steak and biscuits, and lots of Irish whiskey with coffee. All of this starts around 9 AM. By noon, we would be snookered. The main requirement for entrance was that you wear green. Daisy and Carl Swarts were two of my best buds. I met Carl through the newly established American Legion, and they frequented Bell Cove. Carl was from St Louis, was catholic, quiet, and beamed at Daisy's constant antics. Daisy was and still is one of my favorite "trips." She was Jewish by family, had short red hair, wore spike heels, and was brassy with a sharp tongue. I did and still adore her. Two recall stories, and both at parties at my house. Remind you, my stipulation for the St Patrick's party was to dress in green. Daisy appeared at the door in a red dress! Daisy, you know the rules? She proudly flashed green panties right there on the doorstep, and I had no choice but to let her in. I was proud to show off my newly developed lower level, doubling my living spaces and purposely separating the bar downstairs and the food upstairs. I don't totally remember what transpired, but someone was saying a blessing upstairs. It was church mouse quiet, and Daisy was not aware of the solemn atmosphere upstairs. There were several friends here who worked for Federal Express. When being introduced and meeting a new friend, she screamed at her top longs, "JUST HOW MANY FUKING PEOPLE ARE HERE THAT WORK FOR FED EX!". You could have heard a pin fall a mile away. I have a good story about my training Daisy to show proofs, driving brother Jim's jalopy Cadillac, and bring down to East Nashville with a diamond ring on every one of her fingers! That story will have to wait. Like with Joy, I would need a chapter on Daisy and Carl to expound on my feelings for them.

Sara and Harry McGonigal had a trailer on the lot three houses over. They resided in Donelson. Sara was an officer for the Saunders Office Machine, and Harry was a Metro Fireman. They had tragically lost their only child, Kathy, in a traffic accident in the early 60s. Kathy was a talented musician and the apple of their eyes. They had lost interest in the lake for several years, but secretly, Sara wanted to come back. She constantly scanned the newspaper to see if any listings were listed. To her surprise, 148 Sunset appeared. This was the home of entertainer Bobby Seymour, and it was right next to their summer trailer. Sara called Francis Alderson, our neighbor, and a realtor. Sara told her that she wanted to buy the house. Francis said she would arrange a tour. You would have had to have known Sara, but she replied, "I don't want to see the house; I want to buy it!" Buy it, they did. We met shortly after and became dear friends that lasted both their lifetimes. We went to the Bahamas and Hawaii twice and co-founded the Ray Cash Memorial American Legion Post #245. At different times, the three of us served as post commanders. They helped in 1976 at the farm to pick and process grapes to make our family wine, The Recipe. They adored my mother and fell in love with Uncle Boy. And Aunt Berley caned some chairs for them. They were like surrogate parents to me, and they felt the same devotion to me. Harry was a crusty former Navy submariner and heavy beer guzzler. She wed right out of high school, married a Marine, and was widowed less than a month later. Her brother was killed in the war in about the same period. Against her parents' wishes, she enlisted in the Marine Corps. They both had the most generous and giving hearts of anyone I ever knew. Sara could give Harry hell but would die in his defense even when he was wrong. I made life-lasting friends through them. DeLacy and Rich, whom I traveled with, photographed their wedding. Dee, his niece, and I became lifelong friends, and she is one of my "soulmates." I became friends with all of their families. I am a much richer person to have known them, and I miss them every day.

Behind Kate was an "A" frame house. It was available for sale at the same time as 156 Sunset. It didn't have the acreage and couldn't have a dock because of the constant wake from the dam. Ted Hacker of Dr. Hook fame and his new wife Elaina purchased it shortly after I closed on mine.

My other special neighbors were Jim and Nellie Freeman, Willard and Frances, Mrs. Steele, Nick Sedivi, and Nick Jr. On the hill was Miss Gladys, who took over my seamstress's needs from Ms. Wiggers. There was also Edith, Mr. White, Buck's father. Next to Edith was the Sherriff Sutton's fishing cottage and the ancestral Rush house for whom the subdivision is named. Behind the Hewitt's house was a historic log cabin. It was owned by entertainer Mickey Newberry. Shane Dolan lived there as a house sitter. Mickey had married Ms. Oregon and lived near Portland. He had to maintain a Tennessee address for his music empire. He and I became friends. He called me Payne. He had chronic seasonal allergies. This was before many of the medications became over-the-counter. He was constantly coming to Nashville without any meds and would not be here three days before calling me for backup. I guess he remembered those kindnesses because when he moved permanently to Oregon, he called me to come over. "Payne, I bet you are the only person I know who would drink Sake." "Yes, Mickey, I do like Sake." He presented me with the most beautiful 12 sets of hand-painted sakes in a wooden box. "Payne, the Mayor of Tokyo gave this to me at the Japan Songwriters Convention for winning second place." I was so thrilled with it and had to guard it while riding on the lawn mower. I came home and caressed each cup and then thought to myself. He said 2nd place. I couldn't stand it. I got back on the tractor and knocked on Mickey's door. "Mickey, you said 2ndplace. Who was first?" "That little potbellied son of a bitch, Paul Williams!" I remember the song and it was possibly Evergreen, which was made famous by Barbara Streisand. Shane and I became friends. She was a paralegal in Nashville. She was very eccentric but had the best, driest sense of humor that I often yet copy to date. Her classic was if she loved and adorned something, "she was going to be buried with it!", just like the Egyptians.

Rich died, and Elrita moved to Park Place, a retirement home in Hendersonville, and lived there comfortably in her last years.

Jimmy and Marci bought the house from the Hewitt estate. He was still in the tour busing industry. Jimmy has the folksiest charm that people adore and can "milk" it to the hilt. A true born salesman is he. They had an adorable young son, and we all became fast friends. Marci was/is talented and beautiful. Her sights were higher set from Sunset Drive. She was a skilled barber and could exude class with her killer petite body, infectious smile, and brains to boot, which were not indicative of most blonde stereotypes. I was able to get her hired at American Eagle, which allowed her to travel freely. She and I are still close friends.

Christmas at the Manner, for me, has continued like those growing up at the farm. I bake several loaves of banana bread for family and friends and put the tree up on Thanksgiving weekend. Now, normally, it is up to March, but not because of my extending glee. I cannot get it down without help. I still love to cook and entertain, like always. Since all my siblings are gone, it is rewarding to have nieces and nephews to share Christmas Eve and Day. Since my travel days have waned, I spend New Year's Eve at home. I usually ice down a bucket of good champagne and put out the traditional 12 grapes. As a rule, I can barely stay awake until midnight, and the champagne is not opened until March and made into mimosas.

One New Year's Eve at home stands out. Cousins Laura and Doug were in town from Atlanta for the holiday. They were joined by their friends, Miriam and John from London, who were touring the south for the first time. They had worked together in London on a project and became lifelong friends. John was an international contractor who worked all over the world, so I invited them out for drinks. We had a wonderful rapport, and Laura and Doug had to return unexpectedly to Atlanta. I offered to show them more of the sites. The other prepaid suite is now vacant, and they invited me to spend the rest of my time with them in Nashville. It is New Year's Day, and most shops are closed. During our excursion, someone asked what I normally did for the day. I replied that I made black-eyed peas or hopped John with cornbread. I was amazed that neither of the world travelers they were had ever heard of that. Miriam dispatches John and me back to the Manner. I packed my Dutch oven, black-eyed peas, and ham hock, even with salt and pepper, and a cast iron skillet complete with buttermilk and corn meal. We have everything needed for my yearly tradition. As I was taking charge of their hotel room kitchen, I realized I had forgotten eggs for the cornbread. John and I went to several local markets to no avail. Finally, I was about to concede defeat that I had screwed up, but John was determined, if necessary, to drive back to Hendersonville. Passing Johnny B's Grill, I said "John, wheel into here". I went inside with full gusto! I asked for the manager and told them of my plight, dropping names like crazy. I have two "Limmies" visiting from the U.K., and they don't know what the cornbread is, etc., etc..... could I please buy two eggs? The yearly ROPE awards were held at the bar, and I gained a bit of insight. The manager disappeared, and I thought he might be calling the police, but he reappeared with four eggs. I only needed two. He wouldn't take any money for the eggs and said it was a good "detente" for our countries. I was showing them the sites of Music City when suddenly, out of the blue, Miriam said, "Jack, are there many furriers in Nashville?" We were near Green Hills at that time, and I told her, "yes, several!" At the first store we stopped, she put on the most gorgeous full-length mink coat. She modeled it, asked a few questions, and then told the salesman she would think about it. We proceeded through several other stores and ended up driving to see the mansions in Belle Meade. I told them that Belle Meade was our upscale borough. I could see, however, that a coat was still on her mind. At the first store we stopped, she tried on several more coats. Much to John and my amazement, or maybe it was a relief, we were tired of shopping, and she said, "I'll take this one". It was a beautiful fur coat. As we were driving back to Opryland, John and I could almost taste our first cocktail, but glad we had spent the afternoon appeasing Miriam with the furriers. Near Vanderbilt on the West End, Miriam asked Jack how far away from that first shop we visited was. We were near 21st Ave, and I said "less than 2 miles". "Do you mind? I want to look at that coat once more." I don't remember if she tried it on again, but she bought the coat on the spot. We then paraded down Lower Broadway, going honkytonk to honkytonk. Miriam was twirling in her coat while John just grinned and beamed. I still tease Miriam to this day about buying two mink (fur) coats within one hour.

Nino, from Venezuela, married Wally. Tara, and Billy bought Gladys brick on the corner. The Sheriff is gone, as are Nellie, Jim, Frances, and Willard. Eric purchased Mr. White's cottage. Buck has moved to live with Ricky and Sharon, but he can still perform a mean "San Antonio Rose" every weekend on Saturday night Opry. Peggy, Marci's mother, revamped Ms. Wigger's "mother-in-law" apartment at the Hewitt house, and it is now at Red Cedars Glen as well as Anne West. Chance H. now lives next door in Nellie's house. The Steeles, Robin, and Steve Tutor have also moved. Gone but not forgotten is Bill. Forrest, his son, has married Tina and now has both houses on the corner next to the marina. E.K. and Tammy have Frances and Willard's house. E.K. manages Anchor High Marina, and he and Tammy are saints.

Earline and Dale purchased the Hewitt house next door from the Holmes. Our first meeting occurred years before we became neighbors and friends. It was prior to 1996, before I moved to Georgia. A bunch of us "river rats" fortified with a case or two of beer had locked through the dam for a river pilgrimage to Riverfront Park. Quincy Rucker considered himself a commodore and skilled mariner! He came from the old black moneyed dairy farmers of Ashland City and was somehow related to Barry Gordy's daughter. The story kept changing, and I couldn't get a handle on the story. June "The Attila the Hun" Peeples particularly likes Quincy for his compliments. She got mileage out of his saying, "I like your silk pants". Can't Quincy know the difference between polyester and silk? There is God that saved me from doom and drowning more than once on the Cumberland; much like a canoe trip (three days before 2nd full knee replacement surgery 20 plus years later with Hugh), I digress. Dale and Earline were having problems mooring "Lennie Two" at Riverfront Park. On the calmest day, there is under tow turbulence at the tie-up pier at Shelby Street Bridge. After we offered our assistance and got them successfully moored, they invited us for wine. Long story short, Dale asked where we were from. I told him Sunset Drive, Hendersonville, and he informed me that he had just purchased Mickey Newberry's cabin that day and that we were neighbors. I hardly saw them during the Atlanta years. I wish to think we have since made up for the lost years. We have shared memories of their grandchildren growing up, as well as my nieces and nephews who visit. We have bonded with our extended families. Brenda and Joey are almost like "kin," and I look forward to sharing with them yearly. Joey's "beer can chicken" is legendary. I could not have been more flattered several years ago; they elected to spend Christmas with me and my family. Earline and Dale come to their lake house on weekends from their Nashville home after returning from wintering in Florida. Earline and I both like flowers and like to garden. Her favorite color is white, and she always includes at least one white flower when planting flower beds. I have found that true with much more contrast, especially at night. I was not taught that jewel of wisdom in Master Gardener's program. The cereus cactus only blooms at night. It is a desert plant and may go for years without blossom. My "Babe in the Manger" winters in my greenhouse, and I bring it outside past frost. This is an ideal period of hibernation in a cool and damp environment. One summer, what promised to have several blooms for the first time, I put Earline on alert. They were at their lake house for the weekend. I didn't have a clue what time it would bloom. I surmised near eight PM. Dale, always the trouper for our antics, was up for the party. Here they came, with a couple of bottles of (Clos Du Bois) their private stock to await the show. After one bottle had been polished and no near sight of the "opening," Dale said he had had enough and retreated home. He was/is a wise man. Nine o'clock goes by quickly. After the two host bottles were finished, I am now working on my limited wine supply. It's ten PM, maybe eleven. Now, is our pilgrimage to Mecca! You get the picture. Earline has far too much class to ever reveal if Jack Daniels was involved. The beautiful night-blooming cirrus is a sight to behold. It has a strong sandalwood scent. It looks like a cradle with a child nestled in a white cluster of flowers with an iridescent crown hovering. We see and are amazed with omnipresence. Impressed, Earline went home when the flower finally bloomed. The next day near noon, I- with crossed eyes, amble my way down to my dock to have coffee and work the Sunday crossword. I glance over to my left and see Earline equally feeling the "hair of the dog," and she, without any ado, looks over and speaks. "Jack, "baby Jesus" kicked my ass last night! I simply nodded yes. Most of this account is true. Yearly, at their holiday office party, I am asked to tell this yarn, and I always embellish it to the hilt. What can I say about Earline and Dale? They are class acts. We all share values for privacy. One evening, I was sitting on my patio. It is heavily covered in the summer months with plants that screen me from the lake. Dale assumed I was home alone and peered from the side of the patio. Peggy, Hubert, and I are having cocktails on the patio. Abashed that he has intruded on the company and perplexed for words, Dale looked like he had been hit with "a blabbed." (Kindly refer to Harry McGonagall to get the definition of a blubber). For impromptu, "Jack, can I borrow $1000.00 thousand dollar?" Equally, I am stunned, not by Dale dropping by unexpectedly but at the bazaar's request. "Yes, Dale, I can give you a check, or I can go to the ATM!" Over my back, Hubert has pulled out his wallet and is counting one hundred dollars in bills, as I might count ones. "Dale is one thousand enough?", chimes Hubert. FUNNY. Dale was now totally ashen with embarrassment. He was doing stir fry, needed an onion, and didn't want to go to the market for such. We shared many meals. Once, I had a family gathering, making a fish fry complete with a large pot of corn on the cob. The oversized container tipped over spilled the corn all over the yard. Dale jumped into action, ordering a hose to wash the corn bilking orders like a good sergeant. Corn was returned to the pot, and disaster diverted. Pam Bevill still attests that she and Dale saved the party.

No mention of Maui Manner could be made without the name Lola. What began as an eye, nose, and mouth that was gifted to me as a birthday present mushroomed into an art form. Evelyn Smalls, a constant at my afternoon cocktail parties in the 90s and after polishing off two or three bottles of Pinot Griego, became creative. Pursuing the tree, she suddenly whipped out of her purse a vial of the richest red fingernail polish, and before I knew it, she was coating the lips of the tree. That started it. Swap grass was imported from New Orleans, and over the years, Lola metamorphosed from plain sight to an international sensation.

Muster

Jack Payne

LARRY MCCORMACK / STAFF

Jack Payne and his niece Kelly Short enjoy their conversation on Jack's dock on Old Hickory Lake. Jack calls his home on Sunset Drive Maui Manner.

Lola

Jack Payne

Lola

Lola

St. Patricks Day Party at Maui Manor

Chapter Thirteen: Keepsake Portraits

December 16th,1981, getting close to the holidays and having not done much work for a year, I was pretty much seeking out any job and had resolved that after Christmas, I would humbly go back on the road with Bel Air Studios. Keepsake studios had an advertisement in the Tennessean for a high-volume photographer for their Nashville operation. I put on my three-piece navy-blue Bill Blass suit and went for it. I interviewed with Jim O'Donnell and Jim Jenkins. They had several studios and were headquartered in Atlanta. Telemarketing was not the intrusive harassing tactic it is today. Back when everyone wanted to get a "deal," and they had a sure-fire winner. They had rented near the studio an office with a bank of telephones to operate a "boiler room". A manager oversaw a number of people, 8 to 10, mostly bored housewives, school kids, or retirees wanting to make some extra money. They read from a script and the idea was totally based on volumes of calls. They drew minimum wages and had to sell a quota to maintain employment. Call enough people and someone is going to take the bait. The script didn't deviate word for word and went something like this. "Good afternoon, is this the lady of the house? This is Susan with Keepsake Portraits. Today, we are running a special in your neighborhood. If you can successfully name today's question, you will win a 35-millimeter camera and 2 (two) 11 x 14 portraits from Keepsake Portraits for $14.95. Are you ready for the question?" The question was some trivia or current events from the daily news and certainly was not rocket science. The cameras were ordered in volume from Taiwan by the caseloads and cost approximately 25 cents each. They did work, but certainly, the value was in the portraits and the gimmick to get people into the studio and be photographed. A delivery driver was on standby and, again, usually a high school kid or older retiree. They would hand deliver the certificate to the home, collect the $14.95 and instruct the buyer to call Keepsake for an appointment for the first sitting and a 2nd sitting to follow 6 months later. One would be surprised who would bite.

Politicians, entertainers, every possible spectrum of society from Belle Meade to north Nashville bought the bit.

The studio was located at 1007 Murfreesboro Road. One block from Thompson Lane and then the most travelled intersection in the city. Thousands of vehicles passed daily by the studio. The area was not as transitional then with crime and vice as it later became.

Jim O'Donnell was a tall, thin, brash man, probably in his mid-40s. He was from San Francisco and had a very cocky air. He identified himself as Jim, asked a series of questions, had I ever used a SLR (single lens reflex) camera, etc. and excused himself and said he would be right back. I didn't really get a grasp of his appearance and then Jim Jenkins comes into the room. He was shorter, however, about the same age and dress. I didn't differentiate at the time that it was not the first Jim! He was blown away that I was part of the Bel Air Studios operation, whom he knew a great deal about, and that I knew most of the corporation bigwigs that make up the photography industry. I was hired and asked to watch the photographer in action. After a point, to get the grasp of the operation, I was asked to sit with the proof consultant to see her in action. She said she hated her job people and ran about a 29-to-30-dollar average. It was clear she didn't have a grasp for the sales job. I even inputted a couple of suggestions for her. Anyway, the next day I showed up for work, Jim was in the camera room, doing the photography and the sales consultant had quit without notice. He asked if I wanted the job. Long story short, I sold a thousand dollars or more worth of portraits and maintained that daily for weeks, each time also getting a $100.00 daily bonus plus the commission. Even in my glory days of trekking across the country with Bel Air, had I ever made that kind of money? Plus, I was sleeping in my bed at night. My illusions of going back to Bel Air waned, and I had a great Christmas. I had a very good run with the two Jims and purchased the studio from Jim Jenkins on Sept 18, 1984.

Over the years working for the two Jims as manager of Keepsake Nashville, I developed many good friendships and lasting relationships. Lillie Holland was a unforgettable character. She was ahead of her time. She was from an old Springfield family. She was tall, thin, and even in her 70s, always elegantly dressed, usually in high heels. She had beautiful gray hair that gave her even more poise. Her sense of humor was sometimes dry but always witty. She had travelled extensively and photographed many famous people, including, for one, President Eisenhower at the National Golf Tournament in Augusta, GA. Years later, she had many health challenges but still maintained working for Nashville's toniest department store, Cain Sloan. I knew her son from delivering feed from the local feed mill to our farm for our horses. I met Lillie at Cain Sloan when I briefly worked for Picture Corporation of America (PCA), one of my many temp jobs. I quickly realized that was not the job for me and saw the anguish Lillie endured coping with their regimented rules. They kept her employed because of the many prominent family contacts she brought to the photography studio. At the urging of the Jims, Lillie was brought on board to Keepsake in March of 1982. I can't talk about Keepsake without mentioning Randy Buford. He ran the boiler room for the two Jims and later worked for me when I purchased the studio. He thrived on chocolate milk and tequila. His girlfriend was Kim, and she became my secretary and did a stellar job running the front office maintaining the rotating card system to get people into the studio to be photographed. One day, Randy called me and said he wanted my advice. I normally left all decisions regarding the telemarketing decisions to him. It seems a matronly, conservative lady came in to apply for the sales force. Her husband was a very well-known Pentecostal Minister with a strict religious doctrine. That was not at all unusual, as we constantly ran ads in the Tennessean for the massive turnover he had. Consisting of a group of many pot-smoking, tattooed and uncultured girls, Randy was concerned if she would be a fit for our eclectic group of employees. "Jack she has the most melodic, honey pure voice". Randy give her the script and let her read it a few times. Give her a try out and go from there was my advice. Randy suggested I sit in on the tryout call as he would patch me through to my studio telephone line. Sure enough, her voice was pure alright. It went something like this: "Hello, is this the lady of the house? This is Mary from Keepsake Port----- HOLD IT LADY......MY HUSBAND IS HOME, HE IS A TRUCKER AND SELDOM HERE. HE HAS TO LEAVE SOON AND WE ARE FUCKING! I WANT YOUR DEAL, BUT CAN YOU CALL ME BACK?" Total silence. Randy said Mary hung up the telephone, folded the script, scooted her chair back, stood up, put her purse on her arm, walked to his desk without looking at him, put the book down on his desk and said calmly said, "I don't think this job is for me". She then walked out.

March 2, 1983, was an afternoon to remember. It was pre-Easter, and our studio was doing well. Monte, our lanky Mississippi drawl photographer, had just photographed a prominent Brentwood minister and his family. In our "brides' room" was a Catholic nun accompanying two Vietnamese orphans waiting to be photographed. At my desk, was an anxious nine-month-pregnant lady viewing portraits of her two other children. Sylvia was in the framing room and doing inventory. Lillie was at the front desk writing up the photography order for the Dean of Women of Fisk University and her family. Her daughters had flown in from college for Easter and to make family portraits. Suddenly, all hell broke loose. Four policemen, two in plain clothes, came storming in, guns banishing and screaming, "THIS PLACE IS BEING RAIDED FOR PURCURING AND ENGAGING IN PROSITION". My office was to the side of the front desk. One officer told my client to get out and didn't allow her to pick up her portraits that she had given me a check for. They cleared out the studio, basically demanding everyone to get out and kept screaming we're all (employees) going downtown for prostitution.

Let's back up. Springtime and election year in Nashville always brought new efforts to "clean" up the city from vice. Murfreesboro Road was becoming a hot bed for drugs and the whores walking the streets and even in front of our studio. Our landlord was getting lax with his discretion for tenants. A call service rented a suite above ours on the second floor. They were allowed to procure a full-page ad in the telephone book with the cutoff date too late to stop publication. The telephone number was one digit from ours, but the address was the same. They were immediately evicted when found out, but the damage had been set in motion with the published advertisement. Tim Mason, a wannabe detective, was assigned to the Murfreesboro Road corridor for surveillance. The Sleuth he was in came into our studio to scout things out. We had two telephones at the front desk. One red, a direct line to our sales office to have constant communication about the certificates. The other is to serve our customers. He asked, what is the red telephone all about? Lillie, smitten by his charm and good looks, said, "All that is to talk to our girls"? Saying nothing, that it was to a sales office across the streets. He patrolled past several times, seeing the hookers trolling in front of our windows. The genius he was, he put two and two together and rained Armageddon!

A year later, we settled for nickels on the dollar, but it never was the same.

I didn't realize the total negative effect of the raid on my business at the time. I purchased the studio from Jim Jenkins in Sept 1984. Jim O'Donnell had died, and Jim was left heavily in debt. Jim was the first person that I knew that died of Aids. My naivety, but I just assumed he was rich and from San Francisco. I had a fair and honest run with the studio for three more years. I relocated the studio to Plus Park Blvd but never had the volume of business to maintain, and the telemarking gimmick was not working anymore. I guess, too, was burned out of the photography industry. After all, I had been doing it more than 20 years in some capacity. I made several attempts to sell the studio and boiler room intact. I had several prospects, but nothing ever materialized. American Airlines had built a hub in Nashville, and my life wish and dream was to work for an airline. Be "grateful" what you wish for.

Jack Payne

HAPPY HOLIDAYS

From

Jack Payne

& Keepsake Portraits

Season's Greetings

From

JACK PAYNE

& KEEPSAKE PORTRAITS

Season's Greetings

From

JACK PAYNE

& KEEPSAKE PORTRAITS

Chapter Fourteen: American Eagle Airlines

Since I was a child, I always had a lust for travel. Not until I was drafted into the US Army in June of 1964, I had only traveled to a few states. Mostly just to neighboring KY and possibly IND. The exception was one summer when I was in High School, Fred, Mom and Dad, and I went to visit Jim and Marge in Bad Axe, Michigan. Jim was stationed in Port Austin and beginning his long career in the military. Marge was from Port Austin, a neighboring small town. We took an excursion to Sarnia, Canada. The port of entry for us was Sarnia, and we went as far as London. I shall never forget Dad being nervous as we were stopped by the crossing border patrol. A routine procedure, the agent was asking generic questions and he got to Dad. "Sir, where were you born?" Without hesitation and absolutely with total conviction, Dad said "PORTLAND!" No Oregan, no Maine, and certainly no Tennessee with it. We all chuckled, and the surprised agent waived us through with the agent having a new incite of a city named Portland that didn't need a state identifier to it. We had a delightful time in Michigan. Mom and I saw the beautiful Lake Michigan beaches for the first time. The Richards were consummate hosts. Dad and Pa Richards bonded and shared war stories of World War 1 in France. The same with Mom and Ma Richards. They formed a friendship that lasted many years with Ma visiting with her daughters to Tennessee many times before her death. Two exceptions that they didn't share: Cooking and Johnny Cash. Ma was a fabulous cook and could hold her own in any kitchen but certainly was more continental in taste than Verline's Southern cuisine. We were seated at a beautifully set dining table, china, crystal and tablecloth with a full spread. After grace but before the first bite, Ma shouted out, "the BEANS, I forgot the beans". Without further ado, she got up, proceeded to open a large can of Bush green beans and poured them into a serving dish. No bacon, no heating, no butter, nothing. Verline was appalled and talked about that the rest of her life! Ma was also an avid fan of Johnny Cash and all country music in general. She always wanted to see his beautiful home on the lake, and I remember vividly going down Caudill Lane and she saying, “Just think, Johnny Cash comes down this drive”! Mom thought was blasphemous and took most of the country entertainers at face value. She loved Marge's family and was a sport with their “worldliness” when they visited us in Tennessee. One visit, I took them on a tour of Lower Broadway and hit the "gin mills," as Marge called them. Mom showed pretty good restraint until we went into Tootsies Orchid Lounge. It was mid-day, and the place was packed, and Ma, her smile, lit up like a light bulb. To get a table, I needed to order a beer and the two ladies cokes. It was a rowdy crowd with live music blasting. Verline sat stoically, quiet but with a smirk on her face, soaking it all in and checking out the morning drunks. She took it as long as she could and finally blurted out, "Im in the den of Inequity"! We left almost immediately before she started preaching. Verline reminded me of Hyacinth Bouquet in the British sit-com, “Keeping up with Appearances”.

I was always intrigued by my Corkran cousins, Dan and Billy's working professions. Flying. To be able to fly anywhere in the world- free. Dan, a Navy flyer, had an illustrious career with Eastern Airlines, being stationed from Miami-Dade, Washington National, now Ronald Reagan, to Hartsfield International Atlanta. Bill started after his stint in the navy, post Korean War. He begins as a flight engineer with Eastern in Miami. Those were golden years for them as he, Floraine, and Dan established the Hurricaine Limousine Company on Biscayne Bay. He later worked for Flying Tigers and several years with Japan Airlines being stationed in Tokyo with Janet and their five children. I would listen for hours about their worldly travels, and even as a youngster in Portland, I knew even then many of the three letter airport codes and the interesting ways they got their names. I envisioned how wonderful it would be to see these places and the different cultures they shared. Again free!

My wanderlust got started in early June of 1964. I boarded a Southern Airways, Douglas Boeing 720 at Nashville (BNA) via Atlanta(ATL) to Columbia(CAE). I showed the confidence of a seasoned traveler with the 20 or so other raw recruits headed for basic training in Ft Jackson, SC. I'm pretty sure that none of us had ever been on a plane before, but that didn't stop me. I navigated the transfer in Atlanta like I had been a seasoned traveler. Thanks to my military two years, stateside and Europe, I flew countless times and used every opportunity to expand my horizon in travel.

I had a successful and mostly exciting career with my family in photography, traveling extensively all over America. Little did I realize then that one day, that would "get old" and become a routine drudgery more than a pleasure. Getting airport to airport, motel to motel, driving endlessly to get to the next photo gig or meeting, plus being away months at time, pales in glamour after doing it year after year. The perk, I did take exciting vacations to Europe, the Caribbean, Mexico and Hawaii.

I never put out of back of my mind the possible excitement of working in the airline industry and flying nearly free to all of these ports.

I was still committed (working) my studio but was getting "burned out" with photography. My heart was not in it. I went on countless interviews with every airline that I could garner an interview. I didn't care what position. I flew to Dallas Love Field for a Southwest interview, again back to DFW to talk to American, Minneopolis for Northwest, Atlanta for Delta, and probably more I can't remember. Every interview, I got more confidence and seemed to have the process down pat. I don't know why I was never hired, but I can only assume I was overconfident, and I know as I participated in the hiring process at Eagle, there is a great deal of profiling and cronyism that goes into the hiring process. The idea was to get my foot into the door. I knew I was not qualified to be a pilot, but I applied for baggage handler, flight attendant, gate agent or ground crew. Anything to get my foot into the door.

America Airlines opened their Nashville Hub in 1987. I could not have been more excited. I had already been interviewed in Dallas and wasn't hired. I didn't let that deter my enthusiasm and knew I had to keep trying. I shall never forget the day I received a telephone call at my office from my brother Bob. He, too worked for Bel Air Studios and was equally burnt out by the grueling travel and being away from home for long periods of time. Add to this, he was married to Gloria and had three daughters in school. American had a stringent nepotism policy in place about employing relatives. He said he had gotten hired that day by American. I vailed my feelings of hurt but congratulated him. After all, I was working near home, and he needed the job more even more than me. It also thwarted any chance of my EVER working for America.

My studio was fledgling, but I tried to maintain it. I had to scale back employees, plus the new location never generated the traffic that Murfreesboro Road made, and the telemarketing angle was died.

Bob called me one afternoon, which made me ecstatic. DFW had rescinded the nepotism clause and would now hire relatives. I immediately updated my resume fired off four applications for employment. Two to American for flight attendant and agent or ramp and two at American Eagle for the same positions.

Mother had been diagnosed with terminal cancer. She could not have been more stoic with her decisions. I shall never forget her, with most of my siblings present at Centennial Hospital when Dr. Frist gave her the news. Ms. Payne, you have cancer and it's bad. However, you have some treatment options... "Stop there, Dr. Frist." (The Frist's are GOD in Nashville) "How old are you?" Ann and I were mortified with what she would say next... "I'm 86 years old, up until yesterday, I had never been in a hospital. I have birthed and raised seven (7) children. I have lived a good Christian life and I elect to die with dignity. No treatment Doctor Frist." Jim started to sniffle, and she glared at him and said, "There'll be none of that!" The entire nursing staff lined up in the hallway when she checked out later that day. Mother was brought home and did live, with dignity, a few more months until September 1990. We children worked out a schedule and never left her alone for her remaining few months.

Between my two day and night shifts I pulled in Portland and trying to liquidate Keepsake, I was very busy. I barely noticed the "cattle call" interview for American Eagle Airlines at the Nashville airport Hilton in the Tennessean. I had not heard back from any of the four applications that I had sent several weeks earlier. Some voice told me to dig out the Bill Blass suit and go for it. I arrived at the Hilton, and there were several hundred cars and nearly a thousand trying to get into the ballroom. I almost turned around and came back home. A voice said “stay!”. I some way managed to squeeze into the crowded room. A spokesperson said, we will talk before the day is over to every person in this room. To my surprise, she said we are going to call out several names. If your name is mentioned, go to a certain area. I waited, and probably 50 to 60 names were called. Some were there, and some were not. I gasped when they said, Jack Payne. They had my two applications for Eagle. There were probably 6 people at my table. I had learned to keep my mouth shut be concise and mannerly with my answers. I had it down to science. The Bill Blass suit didn’t hurt either. The girl interviewing us said we should be getting a call within 24 hours to schedule a blood test for drugs if considered for a job. Everyone at my table thought the interviewer was favoring me! I wasn't convinced. Passing that phase pretty much-ensured employment. A couple days lapsed, and they called and told me to report to the lab. I was healthy and totally drug-free. I had quit smoking to improve my health. I went for the blood draw and was treated almost like an employee. Several weeks went back and I never heard anything back. I didn’t want to harass them, but I did have some contacts at Eagle and also Bob at American knew people. Bob’s contact told him that I was on the hired list. I had gotten what I considered the best job I ever had. I went to work for Stardust Tours on Music Row. It was fun talking to the tourists, I did well with commissions. This led to working at The Park Suites, (now Embassy) and Marriott Hotel as Concierge and Tour Director. I’m ever grateful to Helen and Leo Waters for hiring me, and they know up front it was a temporary job. I told them upfront I was waiting for a report date from AE. They even paid their respects at Mom's wake in Portland. Mom was continuing to wane, and I devoted more time in Portland. September 19, 1990, Bob called me about 4 AM and told me to come to Highland Hospital. He didn't have to offer details. I arrived at the hospital and saw Mom in death. She had a peaceful look, and I didn't get emotional. Ann, Bob and Tom were there. Ann had already prepared for what was to come. She said we would need to meet Charlie at the funeral home at 10AM to decide funeral arrangements. I said I needed to come home and get clothes stabilize my house as I would be staying at the farm for the duration. I also want to pick up a "bell," a white carnation spray, at the florist to put on the front column of the porch. It was about 8AM when I arrived back at the lake and was walking to the front door with the phone ringing. I managed to get in before it quit ringing. This is Bonnie at American Eagle Airlines. Are you still interested in working for us? Can you report Wednesday at 1PM for orientation? Well, Bonnie, I have a slight conflict. I could feel her consternation over the phone. My Mother just died, and I feel her funeral will be Friday at 1 o'clock. If this is going to jeopardize my being hired, I will change her funeral date. Bonnie was mortified and replied with total compassion. She said she would get back with me in a couple of weeks. I was sad but elated. There was knocking on the door as I hung up, and it was Browns Florist delivering a beautiful fireside basket of flowers from Sara and Harry, my next-door neighbors. They were more than neighbors. they were family. At this time, I was estranged from them because of conflicts with the American Legion. I will expound more about that later. The sense of calm and peace that I saw with Mom and the exultation I had getting the job of my hopes and dreams lifted me beyond grief. It was as if she called the shots, and there was divine interference. She could do that? I have seen many people in death, but my mother was the most serene and beautiful corpse I have ever seen. She had not been riddled with cancerous drugs and she actually had a smile. That sustains me to this day.

My actual start date was mid November 1990 at the airport. The operations room at American Eagle at BNA was a circus. There we probably 25 to 30 or more ramp personnel. Most were college students, young guys attended MTSU, and taking the aviation program to learn to fly, trying to get employment with an airline and skip military service. There were a few of us "old geezers" that were just wanted a new start in profession. We older guys seemed to bond together. Mr. Bill, a crusty retired policeman, was our Patriarch. He favored the older guys in many ways and seemed to tolerate the testosterone-filled filthy language of the young guys. There were a few girls in our group, and some could outswear the men. There also were some ladies in our group that gave our operation class. As time evolved, and with two shifts, the younger guys gravitated to the night shift in order to attend school in the day and also carouse after work. Then, there were the bus drivers. With 70 more or fewer flights going out each bank, there were probably 15 buses to fare the passengers to the "little birds," as we called the Jet Streams and Saabs on the tarmac. Like the rampers, the ladies consisted of retirees, moms wanting some extra money, and just plain good people. The gossip and ill feelings among some of them could be brutal. Most of them found their calling, becoming life-lasting friends and will say today it was more like family and the years at Eagle and were the best years of their lives. The bus drivers also had a camaraderie with the older rampers. We showed each other respect that they sometimes didn't share with the young guys. I totally agree that it was the best years of my life.

I was 47 years old. I was thin, tanned, still had black hair and very healthy. I couldn't have been happier. I had total freedom from photography and the pressure of running a business. My family thought I had lost my mind that I would, at my age, start at near minimum wage a new profession. For years, I would not take a camera on a trip, even on an exotic adventure. I was packing bags in the cargo hull, meeting the incoming and helped deplane the passengers, and same procedure with the outgoing planes. It was total freedom. I took my job very seriously and was an excellent ramper and very popular with the pilots and crew members. My conscientiousness for getting the planes out on time proved badly one day as I was dispatching a Jet Stream, and the hydraulics on the 300-pound door failed. The door fell, hitting my back and knocking me to the ground. Stupid me, I was more concerned about getting the plane dispatched than going to emergency. This was an unwise decision for me as it triggered arthritis and injury to my L5 vertebrae. It was not documented as an injury, and I continued to work the rest of the shift. This was the first of two injuries while working.

I was a ramp agent for at least two winters. It was probably January or so, and it had been bitterly cold. It dawned on me one day the crew chiefs are riding around in heated trucks and air conditioning in summer and don't do any manual labor. They have a great deal of responsibility. I talked it over with Terry, our ramp manager, and he agreed that I should become a crew chief. Crew chief didn't earn that much more money. The responsibility was far greater. They had to account for every delay, deal with lax rampers, plus ensure every flight was successful.

I helped organize several "fundraisers", a meal in our breakroom to raise money for employees that had accidents and were not able to work for a period of time. This was a collective group of employees and many people donating food and their time to help. Because of this, our Manager Radney Robinson and upper management chose me to represent American Eagle and American Airlines to be a Loaned Executive to the United Way. I was loaned to Vanderbilt University and Medical Center. I had my own office at Vanderbilt and actually was considered one of them for the 3 months. I got to experience the perks of an "Ivy League" type school. I help Sphere head a record amount of money for the charity, and it was good to be away from America for that time. They invited me back the following week, but I declined.

Teri Crone (Baker) our station manager, was a tremendous influence on my airline career. While enjoying the freedom of the ramp, she suggested I should do something more cerebral. Like inside with customer service. Huh, designer blue suits, computer skills, and dealing with the public, which I had done for years. I thought it a good idea and went to DFW for training. Those were fun years, and I made many lasting friends working on the gates. She was a good boss, and we honored her with a calendar, "Men of American Eagle." It was March for St Patrick's Day.

I was working as number one agent on an oversold Saab flight going, God know where, Saturday, April 8, 1995. It was Palm Sunday weekend, and the "natives" passengers were restless. There had been major thunderstorms most of the day, with the airport closing off and on and creating total chaos. There were "little birds" everywhere. We had too many bags and too many passengers. The flight had been oversold, and no one would budge getting off. Everybody wanted to get home. I offered the maximum amount in cash or travel vouchers, next flight out, and a hotel the next morning flight, if necessary, to get someone to take a later flight. Nothing. No one was going for it. After pulling every possible bag and finally getting the passenger count manageable, we were nearing delay status. The pilot was being a dick and not being cooperating. A delay is worse than murder in the airline industry. The cardinal rule we were taught in training, from ramp to gate agents: DO NOT RUSH. I guess I suppressed that mantra, for as I was coming off the plane, the heavens open up with a deluge of rain. I'm thinking, get this sucker out before they close the airport for the umpteenth time. If you remember the Saabs, I think they had maybe 33 seats. BNA didn't have jet bridges on concourse D. There were approximately 10 steel steps down to the tarmac. As I was on the top step, I tripped and rolled down the steps, flipping over at least twice and landed on the concrete tarmac on my back. I was temporarily knocked out. Lording over me was the crew chief, the bus driver, plus several rampers. I awoke to a voice on the radio calling management. "Jack is out here on the tarmac, and we think he is dead!" The leg of my suit was torn off, and I was slightly bleeding. I was more embarrassed, I thought, than injured. They helped me unto the bus, and I recall that the plane departed out and on time. By the time the bus got back to the terminal, I was hurting badly, and an ambulance took me to Summit Hospital. X-rays were taken and only showed a torn meniscus with heavy bruises over most of my body. I was healthy and thought invincible. I was driven home and was off work for at least two weeks. No surgery, just therapy. Little did I know, I was developing osteoarthritis that would make me for the rest of my life.

Rumors were circulating that American Airlines was to close in 1996. Bob was more vested than I was and had decided to commute to MIA when it happened. I hadn't made my mind up, but had five plus years with Eagle, had high seniority, and could probably ride the storm in BNA working the smaller planes that would take on many more flights. After all, I had ramp, gate, and ticket experience. In January 1995, Bob was tragically killed in a car accident on Jones hill near the farm. It was Friday, he and I were both off, there was snow and ice, always more in Portland and he had picked Gloria up at work. As they got home, Gloria remarked they should have stopped at the store. He went back to the market, buying a country ham and proceeded back home. On the hill, he skidded sideways and was broad sided by a car snapping his neck. Ann called me and told me the news. Jim was in Tampa for a convention and I was able to get him a next morning flight to BNA. Working the airport was never the same. Ever Kubota at American passing, I would think Bob will be on it. I muddled through the year and made the most of it but missed waving at him almost once weekly.

Spring of '96, I was working a flight and got a call from Teri to come to her office. Usually, being summoned on the radio meant trouble. After work, Teri said... "You go to ATL and lot, and don't you have a business there?" "Yes, my brother Jim owns World Portraits, and I moon light working to supplement my income." "Jack ATL are staffing for the summer '96 Olympics. They want three agents from BNA. Would you consider?" "I'll think about!" "Jack, you will be with American, the parent company, get profit sharing more salary, it's a win-win situation for you...You're going!!!!!!" Seeing the writing on the wall with the impending closing, I would make more money, establish a retirement fund, plus work for Jim seemed like a good idea.

Now, what do I do about Maui Manor?

American
Eagle
Flight Departing For Time
4639 RALEIGH / DURHAM 2:00
4533 ATLANTA
4523 TUSCALOOSA
4575 HUNTSVILLE
may the
Irish

Chapter Fifteen:
Atlanta / American Airlines / World Portraits

January 1996, I made the decision to go to Atlanta; I had no idea what to do with my home. I was used to sleeping in my bed each night and had put my heart and soul into improvements, both inside and out. I knew I could live in Atlanta with Jim until I got settled. I had two weeks' vacation scheduled, and it would allow me time for the transition to move. Kelly, Paula, and I were the three doing the move to ATL. We flew down for one day to surmise the situation. When we returned, we were told we had less than a week to relocate. I posted a bulletin in our break room and was hoping to find someone that would rent my home. God sent an angel to me: John Corcoran. I casually knew him from the ramp as a Saab pilot but knew nothing about his character or habits. I made John an offer he couldn't refuse. I told him if he would treat my home like his, cleaning, maintenance, and grooming, I'd rent it to him cheap. I quoted him a ridiculously low rent amount. However, this was if I could come home anytime, weekends or my days off, live downstairs, and have kitchen privileges. He would be gone days at a time, and we were seldom here at the same time. He accepted my offer. He became more than a tenant. We became friends, and I value him and his values still today. John kept my house in far better shape than I ever had. He would fluff the cushions on the sofa, regularly vacuum, scrub the floors, and admonish me if I left something out of sorts or not clean when I visited. My white kitchen floor always looked like you could eat off it. Four-plus years later, I was able to retire and come home. I was reluctant to call John. "John, I'm coming home. I want you to know you are welcome to stay as long as you wish. With your travel periods away, the house is probably big enough for both of us." John was getting ready to call me in ATL. He had interviewed with Southwest and was scheduled for a final meeting. I moved back home on a Tuesday, and John was packing and moved out the next day to drive to PHX. He is now a left-seater (Captain) with Southwest Airlines, married to beautiful Kim, and raising vegetables in Prescott. He was a Godsend then and a model now for what a

Christian should be. Talk about divine intervention! The XXVI Olympiad was held in Atlanta, Georgia, in the summer of 1996. American Airlines then served only 2.5% of the daily flights. They had daily flights to MIA, ORD, DFW, and BNA. The fact that they had to recruit nationwide from all airports for staffing requirements for the Olympics should have been a red flag. Paula, Kelly, and I reported to ATL in January of 1996. The airport for years, and probably still, outnumbers Chicago's O'Hare as the world's busiest. I believe London's Heathrow (LHR) is third. We three entered into a new world far different from the homey, family-oriented BNA that we were accustomed to. Most of the older agents were tenured, had been there for years, and secretly resented new blood on their turf. They were very protective of each other. I played the "dumb hick" from the country and had a good working rapport with everyone. I enjoyed my ATL employment until I became lame to the point that I was on crutches and knee braces. The arthritis from the BNA tarmac accidents had attacked me with a vengeance.

Jim and Barbara lived in Maggie Valley in Kennesaw. The commute should take nearly 30 minutes to Hartsfield International. When I first started work, they had me staggering shifts. There is no such thing with the airlines as being late. They enforced the "three times you're out" rule. It's understandable, as the planes must go out on time. Pam was so gracious to ride all over south Atlanta with me to find a place. We must have looked at a dozen places, and they were either too expensive or not available. I had posted for a roommate on the bulletin board in the break room and operations, but I wasn't getting any bites. I was getting desperate. I had already been late for work at least twice and knew that couldn't happen again. I remembered from years past meeting Carrol Davis. I had been to his home a couple of times when I was in town. He had managed a bar in Atlanta that I had been to during my Bel Air days. He was older, urbane, an artist, a stylist, super intelligent, and very interesting to talk to. He knew several celebrities and was friends with Roy Topps, who was a dear friend of Sarah and me from the Suzy Wang Lounge. Mr. Carroll considered himself an "unorthodox Jew." He was born gentile, but one of his parents was Jewish. He milked that to the limit. He owned an old brick mansion on Piedmont Avenue in midtown and had priceless furnishings and artifacts strung among the three floors. He rented out rooms to men. It was two blocks from the 1st Baptist Church and Fox Theater. More importantly, it was less than three blocks from MARTA, the subway. In desperation, after another day going from place to place, I saw the Piedmont exit, and a light went off. "Pam, I remember going to an old mansion on Piedmont and remembered Carroll's name. I'm sure it's torn down by now or he's probably dead!" We drove by, and I vaguely remembered it was number 806. It was still there. I rang the doorbell, and Carroll appeared at the door. He remembered me, and I introduced him to Pam. I told him my story, and he said he had a room that had just opened up. I gave him a check and moved in the next week. Now, I knew I had a guiding light! I felt I was finally making progress living in Atlanta. The subway was an inexpensive ride to work until I was on the closing shift, and I couldn't rely on getting the last train going into town. The times at 806 were the best of times. I lived next door to Dan, who also worked at AA. He was also an AA transplant, seeking a place to live. He was younger, had a killer dry sense of humor, but was a "yellow dog" Democrat from Ohio. He loved pushing my political buttons. Last I heard, he is still working for American. One of the other perks of living there was that I could walk three blocks to the High Museum. I immediately bought a membership, and its membership could also be shared with our Frist Museum in Nashville. I had a good ride while living in Atlanta. It allowed me to build up my retirement fund, plus I got to work with Jim at World Portraits. I had precious good times with Pam and her family. I got to take Zach and Aaron to the Fox to see *Fiddler on the Roof*; also, we went to the 1996 Olympics. I had just gotten off the train maybe four minutes before the infamous bombing. It was only about five to six blocks away. The city was wild with constant police and fire sirens blasting for twenty-four hours. Another good memory of Atlanta was when the Titans were in Super Bowl XXXIV in 2000. They played the St. Louis Rams and barely lost. I got to share the game with Pam and David in their home. Barbara was always a consummate hostess and always made me feel welcome, and Pam and David made me very welcome as well. The accident with the Saab on that holiday weekend at AE in BNA was taking a terrible toll on my health. Being the closing agent at ATL could be a nightmare! However, some fellow employees thought it was the cushiest slot. Yes, being away from the “screaming, unreasonable thundering hoard" of passengers, and working mostly alone, had some perks.

Closing shift, I arrived at about 7 PM. Most day agents had gone home. Normally, I worked as the number two agent on the last departing flight. It was international, stopping in MIA and making connections for many passengers traveling to other South American cities. Being number two (2) and closing agent meant I had to leave the post early and start meeting inbound planes overnighting. It required me to walk several hours on concrete concourses. We had probably six gates. It was impossible to be in two places at one time. Sometimes two planes would land at the same time, and some of the ramp crew would not cooperate, which meant the passengers waited on the tarmac, which could be up to an hour. Anger and frustration would be taken out on the first person they saw on the ground—ME.

I was under the care of Dr. Johnston at Piedmont Hospital. He was reputed to be one of the top orthopedic surgeons in the South. He performed an arthroscopic procedure on my right knee on April 9, 1997. He assured me it would give me only a temporary fix for pain, as my knee had deteriorated to what he termed "a ninety-year-old man." I had at least a six-week recovery, and it did help for a time for me to return to work. As I had stated, miles of walking on concrete nightly were taking a major toll on my health. This culminated when I fell out, dead cold on the floor, working a flight. I wore a knee brace and was taking more than the limit of ibuprofen. As the pain was nearly unbearable, Dr. Johnston pretty much said I was going to lose my knee if I didn't have a complete replacement. Even though I was based in Atlanta, I petitioned American Airlines to allow me to have surgery in Nashville and recuperate at home. It was permitted, and I sought out one of the best surgeons, Dr. Garside, in Nashville. The surgery was set and scheduled. Much to my dismay, my manager called me from ATL the day before the operation and told me my insurance had sanctioned the procedure, and I needed to return to GA immediately. After much debate with my doctor battling with DFW, I had a total knee replacement at Baptist Hospital on July 20, 2000.

This was just the beginning of several surgeries, as the arthritis totally attacked my body. Left knee arthroscopic, June 2001; left rotator cuff, Sept 2001; right rotator cuff, Jan 2002; metal plate in right arm, Aug 2007; and left knee replacement at Skyline Hospital, Aug 2007.

I continued to live at 806 Piedmont but was on medical leave of absence from American. I continued to work on a limited basis for Jim to pay my rent and bills. I was limited with travel and lifting, and Pam was a tremendous help. I had engaged an attorney in Decatur, Pagnillo, and Associates to help process my social security disability.

Chapter Sixteen:
Travel

This chapter is a few places and cities that I have visited. They are not in sequence and span 50 plus years from my being in the military to my career with American Airlines.

Paris

Of course we went to Pigelle.

We, about 4 or 5 of my buddies, all green and just off the farm, most probably still virgins, arrived at Gare de l'Est train station. The culture shock was almost immediate. I couldn't believe the circular street urinals. None of us had a command of French, and most people we talked to spoke such thick English that we couldn't decipher what they were saying. We had no idea where to go, but I knew I wanted to see the Eiffel Tower and go to "Pig Alley." We flagged a cab and had our first French experience. It was a very old, dirty taxi. Perfume reeked so thick inside that, even with the windows down, it was sickening. The cabbie was a friendly, outgoing elderly lady. She had to be in her seventies. She was dressed like a lady of the evening, with heavy makeup and bright clothes. She spoke broken English. There were curtains over the windows, and American music was blaring on the radio. We asked if she could recommend a reasonable hotel in Pig Alley. I had no clue what Pig Alley was. She kept expounding on how much she loved Americans and how it was good that we could visit the City of Light, etc. "Ah, Place Pigalle? Yes, I take you to the Eden Hotel." Arriving at the hotel, we paid her and proceeded into the lobby. It was an old, probably four or five-floor, very seedy old building. I remember a three or four dozen red tulip flower arrangement on a table in the foyer. I think it was the month of April. There was an open black wrought iron elevator ahead. I had never seen an elevator like that. The clerk spoke broken English and was polite. "Do you want a room with a bath and girl, or do you want just a room with a girl, or do you want just a room?" I had no idea that Pig Alley was the whorehouse district of Paris. Just like Mom's sage advice coming down the ridge, I didn't listen to her again. I did see the Eiffel Tower and had escargot for the first and last time in my life. I saw the Mona Lisa at the Louvre, toured the House of Dior with foam models of many famous people; what do I see but a model of Minnie Pearland Ms. Sarah Cannon. We were staying near the Moulin Rouge but opted to go to another famous cabaret, Crazy Horse Saloon. It was the first time I had ever seen bare-chested chorus line dancers. I was in awe of the street painters around Notre Dame, and little did I think I would be painting someday "plein air" myself. I purchased two plaster gargoyles wrapped in newspaper that I still treasure. Years later, my niece Kathy visited Paris; she was able to purchase the very same mementos.

Amsterdam

Amsterdam is about 250 miles from Mannheim. It was one of my favorite cities to visit. The Dutch are welcoming to Americans and drink Heineken like water. I was intrigued by the narrow streets, the water canals much like what I later saw in Venice, Italy. There were rows after rows of narrow houses, joined together like townhouses; barely one room wide but several stories high. They had the narrowest steps I had ever seen. Wooden shoes and cheese shops were everywhere. My greatest memory was touring the Rijksmuseum. Seeing some of the world's greatest works was surely an inspiration for me to paint.

Still not too long "off the farm," and like Place Pigalle in Paris, I had heard of Canal Street in Amsterdam. I had heard that prostitution was legal and the whores were protected by the Dutch government. Canal Street is several blocks long and near the Anne Frank House. House after house, large plate glass windows facing the street were adorned with the goods. They each spend much time and money to make their window the one to choose. Out on the street are the pimps to hype their wares. Most had on gowns to match the drapes behind them. Some had beautiful floral arrangements in the window to entice trade. Anything to attract the john! Fred, in Louisville, was beginning to build his Bel Air Studios Empire. He had me often check on German cameras. He purchased several SLR cameras, and I got familiar with the camera shops in Mannheim. I cannot remember what camera I had at the time, but it was a good one. I was totally caught up in the moment and had to have a picture. The light flashed, and so did the drapes close. There is screaming like a murder had been committed. I took off like the flash with the pimp in hot pursuit. There is screaming from every direction as I head onto a bridge over the canal. I was stopped mid-way by a policeman coming from the other side. He was livid and grabbed the camera out of my hands as another cop had arrived and handcuffed me. By now, there are hundreds of people gawking on both sides of the canal. Most Dutch citizens speak English, and while he was stern, he showed a bit of compassion. He informed me that I could go to jail and face a heavy fine. He threatened to throw my camera into the canal. He said if I would, first, give him the film out of the camera; second, go back with him and apologize to the lady in waiting; and third, leave Canal Street and never return, he would release me because I was an American GI. I met all three conditions. While I'm on a traveling roll, I will share about a couple of other trips. Again, some were during my Army days and others much later.

Rome

I was nearing my rotation time, and I had wanted to visit Italy. I was planning this trip solo but had a bit more confidence to travel even though I faced a possible language barrier. I didn't have any defined travel itinerary but knew I wanted to see as much as possible. Whom do I run into at the Bahnhof (train station) in Mannheim, but a fellow guy in my battalion? I casually knew him, but he was always friendly when we met. Danny said he was going to Italy and visit his brother who worked at the Vatican in Rome. He suggested we ride together. I purchased a couple of bottles of Liebfraumilch, and Danny also had gotten some snacks for the 500-mile trip. We had interesting travel companions in our rail car. One was a German actress that had a TV serial similar to Shirley Booth in Hazel. She was going to Roma for holiday. The other was a gentleman from Bombay; he had on a turban and spoke better English than me. All four of us had something to contribute to the party. The actress taught me how to sing "Volare" in Italian.

The train trip allowed Danny and me to become closer friends. We stopped in Florence and toured the city and saw the beautiful statue, David. When we arrived in Rome, Danny's brother, Father Boberg, who had attended college in Rome and worked for the Vatican radio, was dressed in a Roman priest cassock, and trailing him were at least a half dozen young monks in robes. I had no intentions of horning in on Danny's visit to Rome but felt he too was overwhelmed by the majestic setting. I asked the Father if he could recommend a pension for me to stay. His reply: "Absolutely, Colegio Del Verbo Divino. That is where you and Danny are staying." With that, the young monks, looking more like bellboys, grabbed our bags and directed us to their scooters. I had been in Rome 30 minutes, and here I am risking my life weaving in and out of traffic. If you think driving in Atlanta or Nashville is chaotic, Rome's traffic was a demolition derby. Cars don't stop for red lights; drive in opposite directions and play, stop, go, or dare. The winners are the ones with the loudest horns and fastest cars. I was scared to death riding helmetless on the back of that scooter. The college was where Father Boberg had attended. It was a beautiful large Roman-style building, lined with date palm trees and built on one of the highest of the Seven Hills of Rome. It was sparse but very clean. It was also free. I can still see and taste the blood oranges, picked right off the tree and as "big as grapefruit." The priest and monks were consummate hosts. We toured and did all the tourist things. I had planned to leave on the third day to go south to visit Pisa, Naples, and the fern 1962. I was overwhelmed with the invitation and couldn't resist this once-in-a-lifetime opportunity. St. Peter's can accommodate over 10,000 people. I couldn't believe the pageantry. Color-coded passes were given to the worshipers. There are several thousand seats near and around the Basilica. Depending on your status depends on what area you sit in. We were very close, within 30 to 40 feet of the Pontiff. The hordes of people that gather out on the square are let in last, lining both sides of the church. The Swiss Guard ceremoniously starts the processional followed by the Pope. The catafalque-like structure was carried by the Guards. Paul VI was the reigning Pope. He was multilingual. We welcomed everyone in at least five languages. He acknowledged the special guests, those bearing a different color than we had. It was a highlight of my life, and I felt the presence of God.

I left the next morning for Naples and Isle Capri. Naples, a naval city, was not nearly as pretty as Roma. I didn't have the guidance of The Holy See with me and fell prey to a con artist while waiting to purchase a ticket to tour Isle Capri. I don't recall the full details or maybe I didn't want to, but it was a slick talker that knew I was a gullible American. Thank God I had my round-trip ticket in my jacket and a few lire to get me home. I never got to see the Leaning Tower or the Blue Grotto, but I had had enough of Naples and was ready to get back to my safety net, Mannheim.

Munich

There are two main festive periods in Germany. I was fortunate to be there for both. One is in the spring at the Lenten season. Fasching is much like Carnival in Rio or Mardi Gras in America. Germans are more liberal with their inhibitions, and an almost anything-goes spirit prevails. Several costume parties are held in every town. I attended a party in Mainz and dressed as a French artist. I had a false goatee, a French beret, a goatskin liquor flask, and an artist's palette with paintbrushes in my coat pocket.

Munich is home to Oktoberfest. It is the largest beer festival in the world and runs for 16 to 18 days. The Hofbräuhaus is a storied town hall in the center of Munich. The hall can accommodate up to 4,000 drinkers, and millions flock to Munich from all over the world. The fest began in the early 1800s and signifies the end of the growing season and time to party and rest.

Basil/ Zurich/ Salzberg

The Swiss and Austrian Alps are the most pristine and beautiful mountains in the world. The people were friendly, and most were bilingual. I saw polar bears for the first time. The Basel Zoo is one of the most famous in the world, and right there in the middle of the exhibit is a replica of the Matterhorn. The snowcapped peaks and green meadows below, with grazing cows, can be seen for miles while riding through the mountains on the train.

I visited many other cities and countries while I was in Germany. I am sure if I searched my memory bank hard enough, I could recall a story from every place.

Is it time for me to come home? I had adapted well to being away from home. I had made friends and was liked by the military brass. Remember though, in 1966, it is the escalation of the war in Vietnam. I had a cushy job and wore dress clothes most of the time. I was supposed to rotate back to stateside in May of '66 to ensure I got out in June. I was delayed a month because all ships and airplanes available were going West. To my surprise, I was asked to reenlist for three more years. I was offered embassy duty in Rome, much like Ann had been tempted 20 years earlier during her Pentagon days. Since I had been to Rome, I was ecstatic. Remember, this is far before cell phones, and it was expensive to call from Europe to the States. I made the call home. Daddy, always few with words, said: “Get your ass home.” I concurred.

The day we flew out of Germany on a Pan Am jet, I was melancholy. The coach service on Pan Am was more accommodating then than first class today on any major carrier. As I mounted the steps at Rhein-Main Airport in Frankfurt, a German band started playing "Auf Wiedersehen." I choked up and tried to be composed, but as I looked around, even most of the officers had tears in their eyes. I mustered out at Ft. Dix, New Jersey, and was on an airplane to Nashville, now an honorable discharged soldier.

Cusco/ Lima

The Mayan culture of Mexico has also held an allure of mystery for me and to know they preceded the United States in history. My renting a Kaiser pink Jeep and tooling all over in Acapulco or visiting Mexico City—probably the most cosmopolitan city in the world that I have ever visited—can't compare to walking the ruins of the pyramids of Chichen Itza in the Yucatan. That is, until I visited Peru. Jim Jenkins and his wife Dana, I purchased Keepsake Nashville, and I went to Peru in 1998. I had never seen a llama in a zoo before, much less seeing them in their habitat like horses. I was overwhelmed by the largeness of it and the calming effect it had on my presence. Just walking the hills, it was inconceivable how they built the houses and temples. It was cool (not cold) enough for a jacket at 12 noon. I didn't have difficulty breathing at the altitude of 8,000 feet. I also felt some satisfaction that I had now visited at least three of the Seven Wonders of the World. I have visited Central and South American countries several times and only recall one bad experience. I was a guest of my friend Marena, who had rented my house during my Atlanta years. Her family lived in Bogota, Colombia, and she invited me to visit. Bogota is the capital city, sprawling with nearly 8 to 9 million people, and is one of the higher plateaus of the Andes Mountain range. It has a lot of "nouveau riche" growth, being billed as the drug capital of the world. Drug cartels are centered there from all over the world. Her mother made sure I saw all the sites and visited the museums. I was on a quest for an emerald ring, as it was my birthstone of Gemini. Every street corner had a food cart. Almost every cart had the most colorful boiled eggs. I had already tested and fared many of the local tropical fruits. They looked like a Mardi Gras, crystallized in shades of purple, green, and gold. I couldn't resist. Not reasoning and with no advice from Marena's family that they could be a week or older, plus in the blazing Colombian sun, I couldn't resist. I took one bite and immediately spit it out. I was already doomed. I actually thought I was going to die. Marina's mom ordered her to the front yard and brought me a lemon as large as the one I remembered from the monastery in Rome. She told me to drink the juice and eat the rest, the pulp and rind. I tried to rise to the occasion. I didn't die, but I was on the next plane to Miami.

Tokyo

Before I owned a home, I had always been intrigued by Asian culture. I have many Oriental furniture and art pieces, including a bejeweled Coromandel screen. It really hasn't stopped there, as I am still a voracious reader of the Asian periods. I have a portrait of Genghis Khan hanging in my living room. In August of 2010, I visited Japan. It was a trip of a lifetime as I timed the flights to a science and was able to travel First Class on all segments. Although I was already facing health issues, I navigated the streets and subways of Tokyo like a native. I didn't find the language a barrier to communication and felt at ease to explore the city, less like being a tourist. I have always tried to be a good representative of America and try to speak as much of the language of the country. I found the people were more willing to give directions if you tried to assimilate. I was appalled by the "shit pots" or open urinals, even in the cleanest restrooms. It reminded me of the circular open street urinals that I had seen in Paris. One of the best highlights was riding the Shinkansen (bullet train) from Tokyo to Kyoto and wondering why America is 50 years behind in transportation. I loved the city of Tokyo (Edo), but if I ever returned, I would go straight to Kyoto.

London

I couldn't dare list any visited cities or places without mentioning London. I have been blessed to have visited more than once. When asked why I like London, I say it is New York City without the hassle. That is partially true, as I never felt threatened riding the tube all over the city at wee hours. My first visit, while still at Western and working in Bel Air, was New Year's Eve of 1974. The most recalled memory of that trip was being very drunk in Piccadilly Circus and jumping in the Eros fountain at midnight. Marge, my sister-in-law, was gravely ill in Jewish Hospital in Louisville through the holidays, and I had decided to cancel my trip. Many nights we shared at the hospital, while she was still lucid, and she persuaded me to make the trip and wanted a certain Royal Doulton figurine, Pinky, Top of the Hill. I had never heard of Royal Doulton but was an expert by the time I returned. It was out of circulation, but I managed to get two (Kim and Pam) and several others. I managed to garner two, and that is a story chapter within itself! Marge lived for me to present it to her, though Jim said she had been in a coma for several hours. She died the next day on January 9, 1975. The most recalled memory of that trip was my being drunk in Piccadilly Circus, jumping into the Eros fountain at midnight on New Year's Eve of 1974. At 12 midnight on New Year's Eve, all public transportation ceases to operate in London. Our hotel was in the West End, and we had to walk nearly 5 or 6 miles. My teeth were chattering and icicles were forming on my ears when we got back to the hotel. David Darring was one of Fred's photographers and went with me to London. He had never been out of Louisville and was impressed with the city. We attended a couple of plays in the West End, and the theater district rivaled Broadway in NYC.

I have been fortunate to visit Edinburgh and Dublin. Being of Irish descent, and with the aid of lots of "ale," plus my rosy cheeks, I can speak brogue just like the locals. I feel the most comfortable in the British Isles and wish I could return to spend more time. There is a city north of London called Witham. I would like to explore it and try to connect with my forefathers.

The Caribbean has also been an allure to me since Sarah and I toured Mexico.

Las Vegas

I have been to Vegas several times. Most of my visits to Sin City involved alcohol in planning. My first visit, I was working at Bel Air headquarters in Louisville. It was the week before Christmas, and everyone was exhausted. It was a last-ditch effort to get all portraits mailed out in time for Christmas presents. Many of us who normally worked on the road would go to Louisville to help out. This effort also involved the annual Christmas party, which was normally set for a few days before Christmas or the Friday before. The Payne brothers could get rather rambunctious when plied with liquor. While we should have set a better example with sobriety for the employees, we too needed to blow off some steam.

Long story short, David, maybe two other people, Sara of course, and I ended up at Sandiford Field after several cocktails for the last flight SDF/LAS. We planned to fly back the next day, but if I recall, we stayed two days. Verline always commanded that I be home after the Christmas party. This was to ensure the tree was up and any last-minute shopping was done, as she never drove a car. This was long before cell phones. When I didn't surface in Portland the day after the party, she was burning up the phone line to Fred. "Jack is in Las Vegas," he intoned! Talk about wrath; she let "church out," and she almost ruined my Christmas when I got home safely by the 23rd.

On another trip, it was post-Derby, and I had a killer white suit that made me look like Colonel Sanders' grandson. I was sitting at the bar playing Keno when this attractive girl sat on the next stool, and we made small talk. She looked at the suit and heard my accent. "Are you from the South?" she asked. "Yes." "Where?" "Nashville." She said she had a dear friend from TN. Long story short, Billy had a friend from San Francisco named Francisca. It was she. Billy was still in the Air Force. We called him and told him we met over Keno.

Another spur-of-the-moment trip was when the American Airlines hub was still in Nashville. One New Year's Eve, the red-eye to Vegas left around 10 PM, arriving there near midnight. Several of us working at American Eagle on the evening shift checked the flight status, and it was wide open with maybe only six confirmed passengers. First class was totally open. Most of us were off the next day or either didn't have to be at work until late afternoon. I don't remember who or how many, but we filled up first class. The cabin crew partied with us, and we drank champagne all the way, arriving at the gate and able to get inside the terminal just as the clock struck midnight. We took the shuttle to the Strip, walked around until nearly 5 AM, and made the 6 AM flight home. Needless to say, we all slept all the way back to Nashville.

I am long overdue for another visit to Las Vegas but have lasting memories of shooting craps with Lena Horne, running into Ken, Loretta's manager, and he giving me the VIP treatment at the "Coal Miner's Daughter" concert. Previous visits included shows with Ann-Margret, Shirley MacLaine, the Liberace Museum, Elvis, the Rat Pack, Wayne Newton (several times), Elton and his red piano, Donny and Marie, Cirque du Soleil, Sigmund and Roy, Ray Price, just to name a few. It's definitely time to go back!

I have been to most the Caribbean Islands and several Canadian provinces. I can count off most of 50 United States and that could be another book.

In Hawaii

At the Pyramids in Mexico

Chapter Seventeen: Return to Maui Manner / Retirement

Queen Elizabeth called 1992 her ANNUS HORRIBILIS. This translates to a horrible year. She dealt with a negative public that threatened to destroy the monarchy. Princesses Margaret and Anne were in constant scandal, with Anne getting a divorce from Mark Phillips and marrying Sir Lawrence the same year. Charles, not to mention his escapades with Camilla, was being viewed in a negative light. Added to that, there was a major fire in Windsor Castle, destroying centuries of art and history in one of the wings. Things weren't much better in the USA with Bill Clinton and his affair with Jennifer Flowers.

I can relate to annus horribilis, but mine personally stretched more than for one year. I promise I will try not to be maudlin. I moved back home from Atlanta the last week of December of 1999. What was to be the best years of my life in retirement to return to my beloved lake cottage on Old Hickory Lake in Hendersonville (Maui Manner) and not have to deal with the hassles of the vicious traveling public was not the piece of cake I imagined and hoped for. I shall expound on the good times, and there were many, later in a later chapter. It had been a battle with American Airlines to gain my social security disability, flight benefits, and my retirement fund. I had to get an attorney to fight my cause. The adage, they treat you kindly as long as you are productive and spit you out like garbage when you cannot produce, is (was) a stigma to have been healthy, basically a perfectionist, and now not be able to do the things you have taken for granted in the past.

I was not able to work even a part-time position, Walmart greeter, or anything that required walking or standing, what with the constant pain of osteoarthritis. Doctors were constantly changing my medications in order not to harm my liver. This was a result from the accident at American Eagle Airlines in BNA on April 8, 1995, that maimed my healthy body. Between the years of 1997 to 2007, I had five (5) joint replacements or arthroscopic surgeries due to a fall from an airplane. To add to this, I had stage four (4) prostate cancer with radical surgery in Jan 2011, which altered my lifestyle for the rest of my life. I had entrusted my health care to Veterans Hospital in Nashville. I liked my GP (Dr. Murff) at Veterans and trusted his decisions. I had always had a high PSA. The Vanderbilt intern doctors at Veterans Hospital insisted I have biopsies to keep this in check. Over the period of my moving back to TN in late 1999 to Jan 2011, I had two (2) PSA biopsies that continued to elevate at an alarming rate. In December 2010, with me knowing something was drastically wrong while Veterans wanting to do still a third (3rd) process, I prevailed, cried out, for another opinion. My answer was Dr. Ram Dasari at Urologist Nashville. He leads in his field and pioneered laser prostate surgery. I would tease that "he had the Emirs and Saudi Princes lining their planes at BNA airport to get an appointment with him." He saved my life.

After Bob died in Jan 1995, Tom purchased the family home. Tommy had purchased the land and built a beautiful home on what was referred to as the "back forty!" J.A. claimed it and supposedly left the acreage, which was not nearly forty (40) acres but woods where Dad burnt tobacco plant beds to Fred. He was partial to Fred and was named for him. We were pleased that he wanted to stay in Portland. Later, he elected to move back to California to be near his family. Ann and I gave him our best blessings. I had been his administrator and power of attorney while he lived at the farm. It was my pleasure to do so. After he suffered several physical maladies (stroke and more) and being hospitalized, with his constant demands from caregivers, it was clear that I could not effectively perform the job so far away. I made two trips to visit him and tried to be removed from the task and have someone local to make decisions. Tom was strong-willed and it was difficult to make wise decisions. This was compounding greatly with stress for me and dealing with post-cancer conditions, and my inability to convince him to move back to Tennessee where I could better take care of him. My doctors repeatedly told me to let it go and take better care of myself or too, I was a stroke candidate. I was drinking more alcohol than normal, had restless and sleepless nights, and felt guilty that I could not do more for him. I wasn't getting the cooperation I needed, didn't trust his attorneys, and had to finally resort to a fiduciary. I feel they plundered his estate and were very non-communicative as promised. This resulted in him being placed in a group home and hopefully finding some peace and calm in the last days of his life. It was difficult for me not to tell him that our brothers, Fred died Mar 2011 and Jim in July 2011. Tom died Jan 2014 and is buried in Maple Hill with parents and my other siblings. Jim is buried in Memorial Gardens with Marge in Louisville, KY. Anna is buried with T.C. at Portland Gardens in Portland, TN. With Tom's death, I have buried my parents and all my siblings. A day doesn't go by that I don't have a memory or antidote I remember from each one of them. God's grace.

On Sept 6, 2013, I had a major stroke while in the emergency room at Hendersonville Hospital. I had suffered from two (2) TIAs back-to-back the previous night, and thanks to my cousin Donna Freedle, she got me to the hospital in time to prevent my having a stroke that probably would have been fatal.

To recap all of this, less than in three years, approximately from March 2011 through to June 2014, I had stage four (4) prostate cancer, a debilitating stroke, faced financial instability, and buried three (3) of my siblings. I end this maudlin chapter of my life but declare like the song of Elaine Stritch from the Broadway show Follies, "I'm still here."

Chapter Eighteen: Move to Red Cedar Glen

Today is the day, August 10, 2022; I turned the keys over to Maui Manner to Lori and Jeffrey Wolfe, transplants from Orange County, CA. They are part of the great migration of Californians to Tennessee during the Biden presidency. I trust that Maui Manner will be as enduring and bring them as much comfort and happiness as it has been to me. The many gatherings through the years, from hosting Easter egg hunts to the Christmas parties, I ponder some of my memories.

Who could forget the year the house caught fire? I had just installed a new heating and cooling system, and it was nearly 15 degrees outside. The blowers were working at full strength. A lighted candle from a plastic alabaster holder melted and set the towel rack underneath on fire. The candle holder was my mom's, who had passed the previous September, and someone lit the candle in the bathroom. If it were not for Phyllis Goosetree and her weak bladder, Maui would be destroyed. My guests were more concerned about the fur coats on the bed than my house. Bill Freedle burst into action and poured a 5-gallon bucket on the fire. We quickly installed circulating fans, and soon it was just a memory except for a 3-foot diameter hole to the ground floor of my house. After the judge fell into the punch bowl from too much of the potent "The Recipe," he suggested I call the fire department. With over 20 guests in my small house, I decided it was a good idea. I called 911 and assured them there was no fire, everything was under control, and please DO NOT send fire trucks, the fire marshal, or even the dalmatian, etc. The operator kept repeating, "We must follow protocol." After I kept repeating, "THERE IS NO FIRE," I heard in the background sirens. What amounted to a fire brigade—10 or more firemen in full regalia, a hook and ladder, the fire chief, and maybe the dalmatian—cut across my neighbor's lawns, taking out boxwoods and leaving ruts in the yards. The good part was that most of the firemen knew Anne West, a guest, and stayed and enjoyed the party.

My St. Patrick's parties were epic. It was OK to drink beer before 10 AM, provided it was green. And, of course, green had to be worn to gain entry to my party. Sue and Jerry Roberts, owners of Creative Florist, provided yearly the 2-dozen green gladiolus or green carnation blossoms that were my center arrangement. Ask Daisy to tell you about her red dress and only gained entry showing green panties. Daisy and her husband, Carl Swartz, were dear friends from the Ray Cash Memorial. I remember the year the Ketlers from Albany, NY came. Sudie was Harry McGonigal's older sister. Ket was a total sport and ordered a green beer to go with his steak and biscuit as if it was noontime. Bill Hosey, an Irishman through and through, a product of Notre Dame, and a fellow RiverGate Mall neighbor, plus Sandy and Micky were always staples at my party.

How could I write this and not mention Doc (Senator West) and his brandied peaches? He treasured his peach trees and would shoot the squirrels. That irritated his nemesis, Rich Hewitt. Doc lived across the street from me and was married to Kathleen. He had a running feud with my next-door neighbor, Rich Hewitt. I don't know who could exchange the most "sons of bitches."

One summer, sitting on my dock, I couldn't believe the sight coming down the cove. It was a Cessna Cub seaplane. In minutes, it garnered a large crowd from Anchor High, the Rudder, and the riverbanks. It sputtered past my dock, turned around, and was going to depart. As it passed my dock, I said to the pilot, "Do you want to tie up at my dock?" I swear the crowd was as large as the Lindbergh landing in Paris. I ferried them to the restaurant and took photos of the unusual sighting.

I got great mileage out of my night-blooming cirrus plant. The lore that it blooms every 100 years is a misnomer. It is native to Arizona, blooms in the spring, and puts out a sandalwood scent. It blooms after midnight and closes at dawn. Not to reveal our drinking four bottles of wine while waiting for it to bloom, my neighbor, Earline Morris, came by at about 9 PM. She was as excited as I was, and it was a topic of interest at their annual party before departing for Boca Raton. "Baby Jesus kicked my ass last night." It was hilarious to see the normally impeccably groomed Earline looking well spent.

I mentioned Earline; they were like family. She is married to the music mogul, Dale Morris, who pioneered the group Alabama and later the Mandrell's and, of course, Kenny Chesney. I was invited to a cocktail party at their house once, and we were entertained by an unknown duo at the time, Big and Rich. You had to listen to them then to know they would be very big in the entertainment business. Later, I attended parties at Barbara Mandrell's log house, as well as Dale's office on Music Row. The best part of living next door to the Morris's was Brenda and Joey, Dale's nephew. They make a yearly pilgrimage to Nashville. They never failed to come see me and spent a Christmas at Maui Manner one year.

Alcohol was also involved with the many lawnmower races in my yard. I always had an up-to-date Murray lawnmower, and so did Harry. I'm surprised the neighbors didn't call the cops, as they normally started near midnight.

I used one of my lives when my lawnmower—two more have been purchased since the race days—went off the 9-foot cliff into 10 feet of water of Old Hickory Lake. What prevented my death was the attached trailer, which lodged in a tree and prevented it from going all the way into the water. My brakes failed while I was at the top of the hill mowing. Gaining momentum, I struggled like riding a bronco all the way down my drive and decided at a split second that the California privet hedge was my best bet; it careened right, straight for the plunge into the water. Within minutes, there was a crowd assembled, and I was knocked out for a second. I only received minor scrapes and was more embarrassed when as many vehicles arrived as the night of the fire.

Mickey and Darrel were also a part of my life. Darrel was my go-to guy and helped with many of my projects. Ted Adcock and Thelma Lou, the plant lady at RiverGate Mall, plus countless others lived on my 24-hour schedule. I have mentioned before that RiverGate Mall played a role in Maui Manner. How could I not mention Barbara Bartmess, manager of the Wig Boutique, whom we called Raw Silk? We went to Hawaii, and all she talked about going was that she was going to buy some raw silk. After dragging us to many shops, she didn't buy a single thread. Paulette, Bruce, Ozzie, and Angie Hunt were also part of our staple crew.

I have mentioned Nellie before and her fishing with Paul McCartney and her innocence; she didn't know he was a Beatle. She and the Aldersons were dear friends. Willard was a craftsman and made his own casket. Barbara works at Clarendale and serves me lunch. Other good neighbors were Steve and Robin, Tara, and Buddy Wilkins. He is now married to Jeanie, and Buddy's daughter, Cynthia, is my soulmate.

My dear friend and neighbor, Shane Dolan, had to be buried with more items than King Tut, and her introduction to me included writers Mickey Newberry, Ted Hacker, and Elana, who represented Dr. Hook and later the Oaks. They were very instrumental in the music scene in Nashville. I had befriended Mickey when he came home from Oregon. For legal purposes, he had to have a Nashville address. Thus, the cabin. He suffered terribly from sinuses and allergies. He would call on the third day here and ask if I had any drugs. It was before they deregulated Sudafed, and he was suffering. I dutifully played the role of his dope dealer. Mickey called me as he was leaving the log cabin after selling it, and I felt it was an obligation. He said, "Payne," as he called me, "Do you drink sake?" I said I did. He said, "Get over here." I jumped on my lawnmower, and he presented me with a hand-painted sake collection. He said if anyone drank sake, it would be me. He mentioned that he had received the set from the mayor of Tokyo for winning second prize in the Japan Songwriters' Competition. I was gushing with happiness. I quickly went home, but after thinking it over, I wondered who won first place. I went back on my mower and asked him. He replied, "That little fucker, Williams." He was, of course, talking about Paul Williams, who wrote "Rainbow

Connection," "You and Me Against the World," and "We've Only Just Begun." I treasure the set to this day.

Woodrow (Woody) Gregory, later the owner of the fabulous steakhouse on Gallatin Road in Hendersonville, and his wife Eloise owned the Bell Cove across the street when I purchased it in August 1977. Brenda, their daughter, along with her husband Buddy Carr, managed it. It was not unusual at 3 AM, closing time, for us to package up the leftover steak and move the party across the street. I never knew how many bodies I would find when I got up the next morning. Buddy and his 6-foot frame would be stretched out on my rattan settee. It was a sight to see. I have already talked about Joy Ford in previous chapters. She purchased Bell Cove much later.

Many memories flood me as I realize Maui Manner was not only a creative name but also a vibe that existed. It was a haven for the downtrodden and lost souls to find refuge from a dull and humdrum life. When I was tense or feeling sad, 15 minutes on my dock, seeing the lake change every four hours, along with the music from the Rudder, changed me into a happy camper. I shall miss that.

I could go on forever, but you get my gist. Life at the lake was a total vacation; but this is a new era in my life. On the second day at Red Cedar Glen, I was invited to join the poker club as well as to play mahjong. Some 45 years ago, at Maui Manner, I was the new kid on the block. I find it again at RCG; I'm the new kid on the block, and the residents can't wait to play.

Chapter Nineteen: Road to "Shady Pines"

Sophia Petrillo, the matriarch of the Golden Girls, 1985-1992, Verline's favorite comedy television show, referred to the retirement home that burned as a concentration camp or "the home." It was the Shady Pines Retirement for Independent and Assisting Living of Miami. I digress.

One of the most difficult decisions I've ever made was to downsize, getting rid of my collectibles that I have amassed since 1977. What with my declining health from a stroke plus radiation treatments, my health was in a downhill spiral. The spiral staircase plus extensive landscaping didn't help. I was falling down a lot and not sure I was going to get up. One afternoon near dark, I fell in my herb garden on the lakeside. Dozens of yachts passed by, and I could see people at the marina restaurant having dinner and partying. I screamed; I kicked, but to no avail. I could only think of the snakes that crawl in my garden because the weeding was beyond my limits. After several hours, I was able to get on my knees and pull myself up. I silently knew right then I had to move. My next step was to inform Calvary. My niece Kim and my dear friend Christy from Oklahoma showed up and prepared themselves for the show. I never realized the "shit" I had collected with my extensive travels: 35 forms of monkeys, 42 ducks from Finland, the Philippines, plus God knows where, multiple elephants, a China shop of glassware, plus enough artwork to fill a museum. After three days and items stacked on top of each other, they retreated to their homes and left me to decide what form of sale to have. My nephew Tom and his wife Kelly were my strength and saw the move to fruition. I seriously could not have done it without them. After a month of passing the buck, I decided on a company to handle my treasures. Linda Marksberry and her husband Roy were my guardian angels.

I had driven by "the home" for years and had many friends who lived there. The drawing card was one level with a private patio entrance (like a motel) and the right to privacy. Even though it was dated, they made attempts to upgrade the facility. Initially, they allowed me to display my artwork in the hallway—a promise not kept and a ploy to get me to sign the lease. Many residents enjoyed the display. My first encounter after moving was ice-cold showers and 100-degree temperatures, 85 to 90 inside, with an inept maintenance crew. They simply were not adapted to handle the situation. They, as well as most of the staff, were simply in over their heads. Only with my showing out and stretching across the manager's desk did they remedy this situation. The meals came with a constant promise to do better but sometimes were inedible. Not a good way to start what was to be my forever home. Always a promise to take care of the problem—it never happened. Never did I realize the lack of regard for my already fragile, distraught nature but get these false promises to improve. I was simply too old and tired to fight the system. As the steady stream of ambulances came and went, it was depressing knowing I had selected my final home. I endured the daily superior management attitude for six months and simply had to make a second move after a six-month period. It has taken a toll, and I'm just now becoming anything like normal.

Not all was bad about "the home," Shady Pines. I had made many good friends, living and deceased, that made my tenure bearable. From a skunky ninety-three-year-old of German descent with his act totally together, with ties to Heidelberg (I shall have to visit Ashbaugh Hill), {Cliff died at Hospice Alive in Nashville, April 21, 2024}, a soprano diva, over 90 but with a strut that would rival Cyd Charisse, with ties to the Greek Isles and Aristotle Onassis, a mainliner from Philadelphia's Bryn Mawr, regaled me with stories of the Kelleys (Grace), to several accomplished artists who had written books, plus a German/Polish first-generation survivor of the Holocaust. Plus, the Yenta—I shall never forget the Yenta. Clarendale has them too! Meaning well but always nosy and with much too much time on her hands. I couldn't give enough positive input to the Community Outreach Coordinator, who saw my point on the inadequacies of the place and attempted to rectify the problems. Those relationships sustained me, and I gained humility during my stay.

Chapter Twenty: Clarendale at Indian Lake

In April of 2022, I decided I had to make a move for my sanity. Clarendale is relatively new in Hendersonville and near lots of restaurants and shops. Indian Lake is the place to be and is considered the new Hendersonville. Clarendale is a lovely place with all the amenities.

I had to move and am just now adapting. As the song title says, “I didn’t find it there, so I moved on.” “My Elusive Dreams,” written by Billy Sherrill and recorded by Tom Jones, David Houston, and Tammy Wynette, suggests my mindset. I have found home.

Although not perfect, it is the closest thing to being a good, safe forever home. I have been here a year. The staff is super, and so is the rent. For now, I am complacent. I have a lovely balcony that is my sanctuary. Also, I bought a lot of artworks and my culled oriental furniture. Pam said it best: “I find like you are home.”

I have made many friends at Clarendale and have joined the art group. Also, I find satisfaction on the 3rd floor on Sundays with a live telecast from the 1st Baptist Church.

Chapter Twenty-One: ALOHA and MAHALO

You are wondering why I didn't mention Lahaina, Hawaii, or the state of Hawaii in my travel chapter? Even though my place was named Maui Manner. My first visit to Hawaii was with Sarah Keeney in the mid-seventies. Once again, I went with Sara and Harry and the final trip with Chuck Miller, an employee with American Eagle. They had declared then that they had been many times to the islands and once more with a stopover going to Tahiti. One S & H trip I shared with them was with Barbara. She managed the Wig Boutique at Rivergate Mall and was a beautiful and self-proclaiming clothes horse. She could have been a dead ringer for Ava Gardner with flame-red hair and was also from the state of North Carolina. How ironic that brother George sat in a diner in rural North Carolina and saw Ava Gardner's body being interred. Curiosity, after the mourners left, got the best of him, and upon entering the burial site, he observed a wreath left that said, "Love, Frankie!" A nod to her ex-husband, Frank Sinatra. She was on a pilgrimage for raw silk. She dragged us into many, many, MANY shops and came home without a single yard or swatch to order. Thereafter, she was ever after called by the McGonagall's and me, "Raw Silk." My last trip was with Chuck. He and I worked together at American Eagle as agents, and he had never been to Hawaii. I had neighbors who were related to him. It was a pleasure showing him some of the sites that I had seen. A first-time visit for me was exploring Little Beach on Maui. Sara had wanted to go on a previous trip, but Harry vetoed it. Little Beach is famous as the only nude beach in Maui and in the state of Hawaii!

That first visit with Sarah, I knew I was destined to live near water. Every time I visited Hawaii thereafter, I made it a point to go to every island. The fern grotto in Kauai was the most awesome place that I had ever been. That changed when I stepped off the airplane in Kahului, Maui. I knew that I had met paradise. I saw the best of Honolulu, frolicking New Waikiki, and on the beach of Waikiki, and touring the pineapple fields. None of these experiences compared to

Maui. Never had I been during double rainbows arcing over purple-capped mountains while swimming in the most beautiful blue water with an orange sunset you feel like you can touch, in the opposite direction with several white sailboats in the distance. Driving the 2-plus-hour drive from Lahaina to Hana, even though just 52 miles, is rated as one of the most scenic drives in the world. Lindbergh's grave is there by a small church. I had the most calming feeling that I have ever felt and have visited every time I have taken the road to Hana.

The pretentious person I was/am, I thought of owning a home on the water. It had to be named. Maui had to be a part of it! Wayne and I had sealed the deal and made the purchase. The first thing I did after the ink was to paint the house trim "Aloha Orange." Sara and Harry had a yard sign that read "Little Hawaii." Buddy and Ginger had christened their place "Kozy Kauai." I decided on "Maui Manner." I made a pun: "manner rather than manor." The word manner was for the method of a relaxed lifestyle, not for the famous "Maui Wowie" that is grown on the island.

Since I first wrote the above, devastating fires have engulfed Maui. Front Street, as I knew it, was destroyed. The beautiful print that graces my living room of Front Street was purchased on one of my visits.

The famous cartoonist Dani Aguila came by the RiverGate studio to get some photo posters. His father was a Philippine politician who was defeated by Ferdinand Marcos for President. I have several artworks by Dani. The First Lady was Imelda Marcos, who was later President and was famous for her shoe fetish. Dani lived in Nashville, drew artwork for *The Tennessean* and *Banner*, and was most famous for his caricature drawings in the Brown Derby restaurant in Hollywood. He saw me doodling and was intrigued by what I was doing. I told him the whole story and my passion for Maui. He asked me for an orange marker and a sheet of paper. In less than five minutes, he drew the neatest rendering for an outdoor sign. I framed it and still treasure it as my first signed Aguila.

In two days, he showed up again at Bel Air to pick up his ordered posters. To my surprise, he had a colored poster, 4 x 5 feet, of a cameraman with the name Maui Manner on the sail. I immediately framed it and proudly displayed it in my Florida room. Now I have two signed Aguilas. I participated in a charity fashion show in Manheim while in the army. I got to wear it and then purchase a Loden coat at store cost. Savannah Beach or Tybee Island is a playground for the rich and famous. During my Bel Air days, we did many churches in southern Georgia, and I fell in love with Savannah.

I got to meet many interesting people, including the famous drag queen Lady Chablis, and sat in the piano lounge at the Pirate's House many times to hear The Lady of 10,000 Songs, who was immortalized in *Midnight in the Garden of Good and Evil*. While in Savannah several times, I met a very wealthy Statesville family. They were involved in many charity circles and invited me to do a photo shoot for a men's clothing magazine. The shoot was next door to their Tybee summer home. I was astonished to find the shoot was at Johnny Mercer's house, who had passed a couple of years prior and was still owned by his heirs. Years later, in the RiverGate studio, there was a wood carving of the photo from the shoot on the Mercer pier. Dani took the carving and made a rendering of it that I cherish. Now I have three signed Aguila works of art.

Writing this book has been one of the most rewarding endeavors that I have ever attempted. It has allowed me to reminisce about good and sad times. I have been refreshed with memories of my youth that I had long forgotten. Being from a small town and having experienced how other cultures live assures me that we are not that much different. As I age, I find contentment now to stay at home and find great solace in just sitting on my boat dock and daydreaming. I guess I found the answer to my peace when I first saw those vast blue waters of Lake Michigan for the first time in 1956. I knew I would someday live near the water.

As Ouiser Boudreaux (Shirley MacLaine) in *Steel Magnolias* said, "YES, I PRAY!" My prayer for you is that this book brings a bit of laughter and perhaps allows you to walk a tad down memory lane of an era that will never again be replicated. For me: birth, strawberry fields, the innocence of a child, becoming an adult, home, wheat thrashings, success, family reunions, travel, retirement, MOST OF ALL, contentment with God.

I appreciate everyone reading what is but a snippet of my adventures (life) chronicles. "PLEASE DON'T TALK ABOUT ME WHEN I'M GONE." — Quote: Willie Nelson. This song, I want this played at full volume as the mourners march out of Wilkinson Wiseman Funeral Home. Mahalo means THANKS, and for now, ALOHA—hello and goodbye.

Photo Album

FAMILY

Jack, 6 years old and Sargent George T Payne

Scott's cousins

Cousin Peggy (Scott) and Hubert Christian

The Lazy B, Sparta, GA

Janet and Billy Corkran

Niece Stacey Christine Payne

Cousin Michelle Hill

Cousins' Gaynell Freedle, Gladys Owen, Ruth Huddleston Pirtle and Katherine Dorris

Cousins Becky Bucolo and Jackie Hyatt Lacy

Cousin Shirley (Scott) and Jimmy Brown

Cousins Lillie (Veteto) and Herman Bowe, Sellersberg, IN

Nephew Dr Thomas H Short, 1989

Lanna Payne Smith and Jack

Cousin Bobby Phillips and Jack, Honolulu

Juanita and George T Payne

Cousin Becky (Witham) and Johnny Bucolo

Walita Payne

Nephew Preston Smith doing Plein Aire

Nephew Payne Smith, interning as a Meteorologist

Carroll Davis and nephews Zack and Aaron Bevil, Atlanta Olympics, 1996

Nephew Brett, Baleigh and Baylor Short

Neice Kathryn Patten and Jack

The Hall nieces: Sadie, Mom Angie, Allie and Sophie

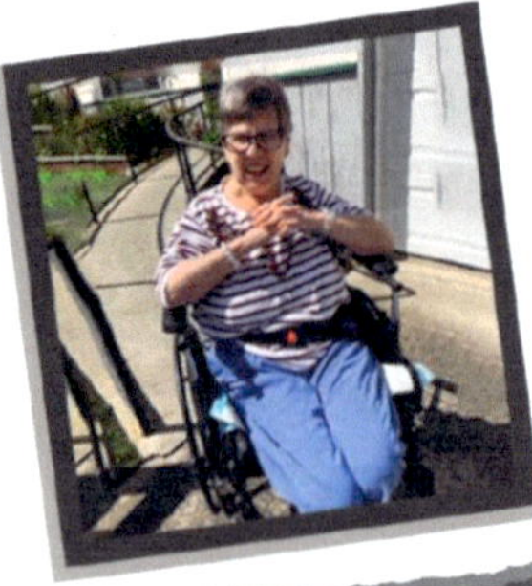

Cousin Amelia Ann Corcoran

Cousins Joyce Witham Hudgens, Mary Witham Thompson and Jack

Neice Kelly Short with Verline's famous cornbread dressing

Nephew and nieces Tommy, Pam, Vicki, Kim, Angie, Jack, Lanna and Laura at Kim's home in Indiana

Neice Laura (Payne) Evans and Jordan

Kathryn, Daniel, John and Tommy Patten

John, Pam, Jake and Ashley Payne

Jack with nephew Payne Smith, and nieces Julia and Olivia Short

Cousin Donna Freedle

Nephew Jake Payne

Cousin Faye Veteto Green

Cousin Daniel Corkran

Corkran cousins (Kelly, Chris, Connie, Steve and Carolyn) California

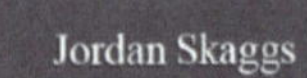

Jordan Skaggs

Kendra Skaggs and fiancé Dr Stephen Marks

Neice Julia (Short) Polk with Tye, Zeke and triplets Shepherd, Brody, and Jovie

Niece Kim (Payne) and Barry Skaggs

Loren Black Payne and Valerie and family

Christopher and Jordan Evans

Niece Kathy Patten with daughters in law Emily and Courtney

Travis, Robert, Kathy Little, Jack and Glenna Vincent

FRIENDS AND NEIGHBORS

Sara and Harry McGonigal

Barbara Alderson Wims

Mickey Conner

Sarah Keeney blowing on the Belvedere

Cece McCarthy and Jack

Chuck King, Jack and Christy Kuhn

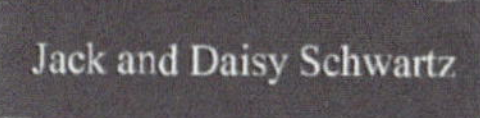

Jack and Daisy Schwartz

Jack with Delacy Layhew

Delacy Layhew with son Rich

John Corcoran and the mistress of Seam, Oralee Moore

Dan Flynn, American Airlines ATL

Bill and Forrest Beavin

Kathleen West

Jack and friend Dee Munoz

Dewayne, Geneva, Jack and Tasha

High school classmates Allen Haynes, Jack and Billy Freedle

Julie McClure and Jack, Fat Tuesday NOLA

Nellie Freeman

Tom Rainey

Jack with Cindy Watkins and Jeannie Wilkins

Lillie Holland and Monte Smith, Keepsake Portraits

Chris Bierbalm, American Eagle Airlines

Hattie May Searcy Wilkinson

Jack's hair stylist Roshanda Mooneyhan

Harry and Sara McGonigal (with her beloved mink coat!)

Lillie Holland and Jim and Dana Jenkins, Keepsake Portraits

Terry Martel, Kenosha, WI

Angie Hunt

Jim Hughes, American Eagle Airlines

Jack with Earline and Dale Morris, Maui Manor

Jack and Barbara Bartmess

Jack and Anne West

Jack with Johnnie Austin

Jack with Kim and John Corcoran

Buddy Wilkins, Cynthia Watkins and Jack

Jack with Linda Meeks

Brenda and Joey Johnson

Nan Harris

Jack and Joy Ford at Ming Wang Eye Ball

Bill Barnes and Carol Andrews

Jack with Cissy Boone, Derby Day 2023,Clarendale

About the Author

This is my first effort at writing. It is a collection of stories as I recalled from the age of 4 years. Growing up in a rural farm area with six much older siblings, I found out quickly that I had to “shine” to compete with them. It must have worked for I was nicknamed Sunshine most of my life.

Death takes the
Body. God takes the
Soul. Our mind holds
The memories. Our
Heart keeps the love.
Our faith lets us know
We will meet again.

Author: Unknown

Made in the USA
Columbia, SC
19 April 2025

d6d376fc-f91a-42ac-b6ff-8078c9e5e549R03